Planning your bathroom

Anthony Snow
and Graham Hopewell

a Design Centre book

Planning your bathroom
First edition published 1976
Second impression 1978
A Design Centre book published
in the United Kingdom by
Design Council 28 Haymarket
London SW1Y 4SU

Design by Anne Fisher
Bathroom drawings by Richard Draper
Printed and bound in
the United Kingdom by
Balding + Mansell Ltd
London and Wisbech

ISBN 0 85072 026 5

Contents

Introduction

The purpose of this book is to help people make up their minds. Decisions can best be taken in the light of knowledge, and knowledge is largely the product of information. The bulk of the book has therefore been arranged for quick and easy reference. The information you are likely to need when planning a new bathroom or rehabilitating an old one is given in alphabetical order under a number of headings. We have not tried to provide a sophisticated reference system because we think that people want to be given information in the way that questions arise in their minds. If you want to know about basins, therefore, you look under the heading 'basins' – and not under 'fittings: sanitary/ceramic/domestic', or whatever a universal reference system might dictate.

Many people will have had the urge or the need to create a new bathroom where none existed before, in an older house perhaps, or to add an extra bathroom or shower room to cater for a growing family and relieve one possible area of household stress and strain. Those fortunate enough actually to build their own house will probably have had the services of an architect, who should have been able to provide the most satisfactory arrangement for their needs. But most of us have not had this opportunity and this book should help anybody to avoid the pitfalls that exist and to achieve a much better result than they would otherwise get.

In the first part of the book, before the alphabetical reference section, we have provided a section on general bathroom planning, as this lends itself to a fairly comprehensive approach. And to show how theory can be translated into practice, we have included a number of worked examples, which range from the strictly practical to the more lavish and slightly less conventional.

The great opportunity in planning your bathroom is that of letting yourself go a little. This is a room that can reflect your personal feelings without offending those of anybody else, but we should add a word of warning: bathrooms are expensive in comparison with most other rooms in the house and, on the whole, they are relatively permanent. Plumbing and drainage systems are costly and difficult to alter, so it is particularly important to get the basic layout of your bathroom right.

Finally, to help in buying bathroom equipment, we have included a concise guide to the manufacturers who make products in this field, with particular reference to those whose products have been accepted for inclusion in the Design Council's Design Index. This information cannot, of course, be absolutely comprehensive or up-to-date, but it will still be useful to anybody who is searching for product information in what is, after all, quite a specialised market and who isn't satisfied with what the local stockist can provide off the shelf.

TIM STREET-PORTER/LIZ WHITING

4

Two fairly extreme views of what a bathroom should be. On the left the designer has really gone to town and, although the period fittings are quite simple ones, the overall effect is rich and fantastic. On the right in the bathroom designed by Broadway and Malyan, the result of careful planning is very cool and chaste, with a back wall like an abstract painting.

COLIN WESTWOOD

5

The overall plan

A bathroom can be anything from the all too familiar minimum of a bath, basin, and possibly WC, all grouped together in an alternately chilling and steamy confined space, to a room a good deal larger than many living-rooms, lavishly equipped and luxuriously furnished to cater for every ablutionary need and many more besides – including making up, hair drying, keeping fit, dressing, telephoning and just relaxing, to name but a few.

In any form, however, a bathroom contains a number of fittings that are difficult and expensive to renew or move around. No other room in the house is likely to be changed less frequently and the kind of rearrangement that would be routine elsewhere tends to be rarely undertaken, if at all.

It follows that, whether you are contemplating the comparatively simple job of refurbishing an existing bathroom – with, perhaps, a few new fittings and decorations – or a more radical rearrangement in an existing space, or even creating an entirely new bathroom from scratch, the greatest consideration must be given to all the factors involved. Whatever the limitations in terms of space and cost, you will have to live with your basic decisions for a very long time, irrespective of any changes you may make to the decorations later on.

All bathrooms have certain items of equipment in common. The alphabetical reference section on pages 69–70 gives details of the types of fitting available and their selection. In terms of planning and design, however, there are a number of general principles that we should consider before going on to look at how the main items of equipment – basins, baths, showers, bidets and WCs – can be used in the contexts of various sizes of room.

The minimum requirement with which we are likely to be concerned is a basin, a bath or shower, and possibly a WC. Small bathrooms need the greatest ingenuity in obtaining the most satisfactory arrangement of the fittings and ancillary equipment, such as towel rails, mirrors, lighting, cupboards and other accessories. Where there is more space available we can consider having the WC separate from the bathroom – which can, to some extent, relieve congestion when several members of the family have to get washed at the same time in the morning, particularly if another basin can be provided in the WC. Alternatively, a separate shower room with a basin can be formed in any space that can be spared elsewhere in the house, or additional basins can be fitted in the bedrooms, to ease the pressure on a single bathroom. It is worth remembering that a combined bathroom and WC will give more usable space in a single room, and may even make space for an additional fitting such as a step-in shower, a bidet, or a second basin.

Although the larger bathroom is less exacting in terms of tight planning and ingenuity, imagination and design skill are equally necessary if a functional and pleasing result is to be achieved. A room of, say, 5·0 × 4·0m with a bath on one wall, a basin on another and a WC in the corner is not likely to be either convenient or beautiful, however luxurious the fittings themselves may be. It will simply mean that you have to walk long distances from one fitting to another and it will look as empty and under-furnished as it is under-utilised. A warm, close-fitted carpet, rather than chilly lino flooring, will not go far towards relieving the situation, nor will heavily patterned wallpaper and curtains. On the other hand, where space is available, good planning and design can produce a room where function can be combined with pleasure and relaxation.

In addition to planning the layout of the bathroom and its fittings, we must also give careful thought to the appearance we wish to achieve. There may be an optimum layout for the needs of the family concerned, but the opportunities that exist for influencing the appearance of the room at the design stage through

This small bathroom has been fitted in under the slope of the roof. A distinctive painting scheme on the cupboard doors avoids a clinical feeling and good use has been made of odd spaces left over to provide neat shelves for extra storage space.
Designed by Rothermel Cooke

the use of different materials, colours and textures are enormous. The fittings themselves are the most permanent elements in the scheme and these should be chosen not only to function well, but also to last in visual terms. Generally speaking, simpler forms are more aesthetically durable, while exaggerated shapes and fashionable colours, however appealing they may be at the time, can easily look very out-dated ten years later.

Similarly, permanent finishes, such as tiling, mosaics, plastics laminates and wall panelling, although they are easier to renew than fittings, are likely to be part of the room for a relatively long time. When choosing them, therefore, we have to ask ourselves how long they are going to remain and whether we will continue to be happy with them. As with the fittings, the simpler the permanent finishes, the longer they will last visually. Of course, if you want to express yourself strongly in terms of the interior design of your bathroom – and there's no reason why you shouldn't – painted or applied wall coverings, painted or polished woodwork, and curtains, blinds and floor coverings are all elements through which a striking decorative effect can be imposed and changed from time to time without resorting to major structural alterations.

Two views of a clean, straightforward bathroom design produced for a housing development. The horizontal pine boarding conceals the plumbing and cupboards while a wall mirror gives a feeling of space. An opal glass shelf running the full length of the mirror hides a long fluorescent strip light – a practical and inexpensive feature that adds to the purpose-built character of the room. Architect John Prizeman for Wates Ltd

The five main fittings

Basins

The planning process must, however, start with a look at the five main items of equipment that we may want to install or replace in the bathroom, beginning with basins. The various types of basin available are discussed in full on pages 28–30 of the reference section. Broadly speaking, there are two main types: wall-hung (with or without a pedestal), and counter-top or 'vanitory' basins, which are becoming increasingly popular. Your choice will depend on cost and on the layout of the room.

The main planning point to remember when choosing and siting a basin is that there should be adequate space to use it easily, with enough room to stand at it and sufficient elbow space at either side. It may sound too obvious to need stating, but the fact is that plenty of bathrooms exist where one cannot step back far enough to bend over the basin without bumping into the bath and where basins have been fixed so close to a side return wall that it is impossible to wash comfortably. In practice, 200mm will be needed on each side of the basin and about 700mm in front of it.

Wall-hung basins are, of course, easier and cheaper to install and they generally take up less room than counter-top basins – particularly the smaller models. Even in a very small bathroom, however, they may not provide the best solution. It may well be that a carefully thought out counter-top with an inset basin will work better in a limited space, tying up all the loose ends caused by left-over spaces and providing valuable shelf space above and storage below. And conversely, the best possible overall layout for a larger bathroom might not lend itself to the use of a counter-top basin; to insist on having one might simply result in having a basin set into a piece of furniture with unusable spaces each side and awkward corners to bump into. The choice, your budget apart, should not depend so much on the size of bathroom as its overall layout. Don't let glossy advertisements blind you to the principles of rational planning.

Apart from fixing to the wall and plumbing in, wall-hung basins require no complicated additional constructional work. Any basin has to be connected to hot and cold water supplies and to a waste pipe, ideally with the plumbing concealed. Unless the supply pipes can be hidden in the wall, along with the waste pipe, some other way of concealing them will have to be found. Pedestal basins, in theory at least, hide all the plumbing, but many of them leave a considerable gap between the pedestal and the wall and the plumbing has to be arranged in a particular way. There is often insufficient room to take the waste pipe down to the floor inside the pedestal and so, whichever route it takes, it is bound to be visible; the result looks like an attempt to hide something that failed. Furthermore, it is often a good idea to keep the bathroom floor as free of obstructions as possible – WCs and bidets that cantilever out from the wall are made for this purpose – and a pedestal merely adds to the clutter at floor level. One suspects that pedestals are, to some extent, a leftover from the days of unsightly U-bend waste traps before the coming of the more elegant bottle traps of today. Another and better way of hiding the plumbing is to build a duct out from the wall and up to about 150mm above the basin to provide a useful shelf.

If your budget allows it and the layout is suitable, you can go for a counter-top basin. There are a number of different models available to suit different methods of construction, some lead to more elegant results than others.

The simplest choice is to use one of the ready-made ceramic counter-tops with integral basins which are made to fit onto joinery fittings. Provided that one of the lengths in which these tops are available works well in the scheme, their use overcomes the problem of building a specially finished top. Ready-made 'vanitory units' can also be bought with a basin set into a plastics laminate topped cupboard or kneehole dressing table. As with all ready-made furniture units, intelligent planning is needed to integrate these into a scheme if awkward left-over spaces and sharp corners are to be avoided.

Fitting a basin into a purpose-designed and built counter-top is inevitably rather expensive because it involves special joinery work and, depending on the choice of finish, maybe other trades as well. Nevertheless, where your budget and the layout permit it, this can be the best solution. There are basins on the market for setting into any sort of top in several types of material. Some are made to lip over the top; these are relatively easy to fit as the hole for the basin does not need to be very skilfully cut. On the other hand, water splashed onto the surrounding top cannot be swabbed back into the basin because of the raised lip. A more attractive, but more expensive, arrangement is provided by a ceramic basin fitted under the worktop, but this means a high standard of workmanship. Any counter-top provides a large area of shelf space and can help to unify the room as a whole. Moulded plastics tops can have an integral splashback to do away with the potentially leaky joint where the top joins the wall. Other suitable materials for vanitory tops include ceramic tiles or mosaic on block-board, marble and terrazzo.

It is worth considering where the basin taps should be mounted. Basins are normally provided with tap holes, although not all of them have these spaced so as to allow a mixer tap to be used and mixer taps may be an advantage, particularly for hand washing. Where the basin is fitted against a duct or hollow partition the taps can be wall-mounted and for this purpose many basins can be ordered without tap holes. Wall-mounted taps look particularly neat and leave the basin and counter-top clean and free of obstructions. If space is at a premium, it may be worth mounting taps on the worktop to one side of the basin. Some mixer taps have a combined 'pop-up' waste device which is operated by a knob between the taps and eliminates the conventional plug and chain, but these cannot be wall-mounted.

Accessories associated with the basin, such as holders for toothbrushes, tooth mugs, and hooks or rails for face cloths and towels, should all be fitted close to the basin. It is worth positioning these and any shelves that are required as carefully as possible together to give the best overall arrangement. For those who want to put shaving and washing things out of sight, a bathroom cabinet can also be provided close to the basin. Unless the basin is unusually deep, however, or built out from a duct, nothing bulky should be fixed to the wall behind the basin that can prevent people putting their heads down over the basin for washing their faces or hair. It is a good idea to have a mirror behind the basin and this should be large enough to enable people of all sizes to use it without bending or stretching.

Good lighting at the basin is an obvious requirement but one rarely finds that one's face is brightly lit when looking into the mirror in most bathrooms. In fact it would seem that the principles of mirror lighting are often not appreciated. If the basin is sited in front of a window, natural lighting will be enough during the day, but good artificial light will still be essential after dark. The clue to the best solution is to be found in the 'theatre dressing room' arrangement in which the mirror is surrounded by bare bulbs that light the face from all directions. However, this is a rather extreme answer in the domestic situation. More detailed solutions are given in the reference section on page 47, but the main requirement is that light should fall on the face from several angles if possible. A single strip-light above the mirror is not really good enough, but if you do decide on this, it should be as long as possible and fitted

A number of details in this unusually shaped bathroom have been carefully considered, including a very neat shower curtain track in the pine boarded ceiling, a generous expanse of mirror above a simple recessed pine shelf, and good ventilation from narrow louvred windows.
Designed by Peter Aldington

11

with a diffusing shade. A 'downlighter' or an opaque shade will simply throw a beam of light onto the worktop and basin and your face will stay in shadow. Strip-lights, either tungsten or fluorescent, on either side of the mirror will light the face well. A more sophisticated solution is to have the mirror spaced out from the wall with strips of opal glass along its sides through which fluorescent strip-lights can shine.

Baths

The second major item of bathroom equipment is, of course, the bath. Baths are now available in a range of materials and many different shapes, sizes and colours; details are given in the reference section on pages 30–31. Shorter baths are less satisfactory in use than long ones and should only be used where there is insufficient space for an average 1700mm long bath. The simplest baths have taps and waste at one end, with the taps being either central or, if it is more convenient, at a corner and these models, being at the cheaper end of the market, are generally sensible, straightforward designs. As in other fields, however, manufacturers let their imaginations rip as prices rise, often with results that are none too happy. Many larger, more luxurious baths incorporate welcome refinements such as built-in grab handles, soap recesses, taps placed in the side of the bath so that they can be reached easily, and non-slip areas for showering. Other 'luxury' baths are a different matter and display fanciful, amorphous and vulgar forms of no practical value or beauty. The increased use of materials such as acrylic and glass reinforced plastics has also tended to bring out the worst in bath manufacturers. But there are exceptions and these are worth seeking out for the advantages they offer.

If you choose a bath that has no provision for things such as soap, nail brush and sponge, these will need to be kept somewhere else close at hand – and even a bath with a built-in soap dish is unlikely to have enough space for everything. Recessed holders for fitting into the wall are a good answer to this problem; they are made in ceramic to match tiled walls. Projecting receptacles are also available in many different forms. A grab handle is well worth having – particularly if there are children or elderly people in the house. Accessories in general are discussed in more depth on pages 26–27 of the reference section.

The bath is most likely to be fitted against a wall or possibly in the corner of the bathroom. There are baths on the market that fit diagonally across the corner of the room where space allows, but it is difficult to see much practical advantage in this, although the effect is a bit exotic. Since they simply take up more space than a conventional bath, perhaps they just serve to demonstrate the fact that one has a bathroom big enough to have space to spare. There may be room, in large bathrooms, to have the bath in the middle of the floor and circular baths are available with this in mind. Such an arrangement may suggest the luxury of ancient Rome, with room for the slaves to dance round in attendance, but again its practical advantages are dubious. Even in an unusually large room the bath may well be best kept against a wall, with a clear space for access about 1100 × 700mm next to it running alongside the bath.

Wherever the bath is sited, care must be given to the arrangement of the plumbing. Supply and waste pipes can be concealed in ducts or under the floor (with provision for access) but it is worth keeping the run of the waste pipe as short as possible to avoid blockages. The walls near the bath should have a splash resistant finish to a height of at least 500mm above the rim of the bath – and to ceiling height if a shower is fitted. Ceramic tiles or mosaic are traditional finishes for this purpose but other materials can be used, including plastics laminates, provided that care is taken to make any joints absolutely watertight. Recent developments in synthetic sealers have made it much easier to avoid the nasty, leaky joint where the bath meets the wall, but this can still be a problem with some designs, particularly if the material of the bath is flexible to any extent.

While on the subject of baths, a word about general illumination in the bathroom. Except in very small rooms where the mirror lighting arrangements may be enough to light the whole room, some additional general lighting will need to be provided. For people addicted to reading in the bath it is as well to site a general overhead light where it can also serve as a reading light. A larger, more exotic bathroom could have a more complex lighting scheme in which a separate reading light could form a part. Lighting is discussed in more detail on page 47 of the reference section.

Showers

Showers are quicker to take than baths, more economical (the average shower uses about one third of the water used for a bath) and are more hygienic because one is washing in a constant supply of clean water. They are discussed in detail on page 52. On the other hand, a shower cannot provide the therapeutic and relaxing effect of lying in a warm bath and in most cases, where there are young children for example, a bath is essential. Relatively few people will be happy only to have a shower and do without a bath altogether and a shower can, of course, be installed quite satisfactorily in a bath. If the bath is to have a shower it should have a standing area with a slip-resistant finish and it should also be fitted with one end against a wall to provide a fixing for the shower fitting. The wall must have a splash-proof finish up to at least the height of the shower outlet. A shower that is enclosed on three sides should have a space 900 × 700mm in front of it for access; an unenclosed shower should have a space 900 × 400mm.

Showers of adjustable height can be used by both adults and children, but if one fixed position for the shower is acceptable the plumbing can be concealed in the wall with controls set at a convenient height. Combined bath/shower mixer tap units generally have a flexible shower hose that can be fitted to sockets at different heights. Thermostatic shower controls ensure water at the correct temperature without the need to 'balance' the hot and cold water supply to the shower via the taps. They are also an important safeguard against scalding where children are concerned.

The usual method of protecting the rest of the room from splashes of water from the shower is to have a curtain made from a suitable material – generally plastics or glass fibre. The bathroom must be planned so that there is somewhere for the shower curtain to tuck away tidily when not in use. As an alternative to a curtain, a glass screen can be fitted to one end of the bath at the side. Some screens hinge to give better access to the taps and for cleaning, in which case the wall next to the bath must be free from obstructions. A screen will often look neater than a curtain when it is hinged in this way but if it cannot be fitted in, a fixed screen can be used in conjunction with bath taps sited independently of the shower control – on the side of the bath or on a side wall, for example.

If there is enough space for one, a separate, step-in shower is ideal because it will provide more space for manoeuvre and easier access. Such a fitting can either be in the form of a complete, ready-made shower compartment or a purpose-built unit based on a proprietary shower tray. Shower cubicles can have either a curtain or a glass door to minimise splashing; in the latter case some form of ventilation will be required, perhaps with an extractor fan and ceiling duct which will help to ventilate the rest of the bathroom.

Shower controls have already been mentioned briefly. The advantages of thermostatic controls over manual ones

A fully-tiled, built-in shower that in effect forms the end wall of the bathroom and is divided off by a sliding acrylic door.

DAVID CRIPPS

13

are well worth considering; they give consistent temperatures irrespective of whether somebody else in the house is using hot water from the system and they are safer for children in particular. Various types of shower arm and shower head are available – either fixed or adjustable – and some give a more efficient shower if your water pressure is not very high.

It is well worth having soap holders and grab handles in the shower, placed at the right height for everybody to use. One useful, though rarely provided, shower accessory if space permits is a seat in the shower that can be used when washing one's feet and legs. This can take the form of a boxed-out shelf clad in the same material as the shower compartment.

Ready-made shower cubicles are, of course, easy to install and come complete with all the accessories built in. As a means of providing the basic facility they have a lot to be said for them. Unfortunately, many of them are hideous to look at and, without skilful design, they are hard to integrate into the rest of the bathroom so the effect is likely to be that of a large and ungainly piece of cabinet furniture rather than a built-in unit.

Bidets

Despite an increased awareness of its prevalence on the Continent, the bidet – the fourth major item of bathroom equipment – is still a rarity in the British bathroom. Its inclusion, as with a separate shower compartment, depends on the space available, but the fact remains that no French bathroom is thought complete without a bidet, even if this means having a shower instead of a bath for space reasons.

The primary purpose of the bidet is, of course, sexual hygiene. Other uses, including washing feet, soaking stockings, and sailing toy boats, are bonuses that vary from family to family. In spite of the relatively low level of demand for bidets, manufacturers make them to match many

WC suites. The different types available are discussed on page 32 of the reference section.

In terms of planning, it is important to ensure that there is enough space on each side of the bidet for comfort – 200mm is a minimum – and 600mm in front of it for access. Pipes can be concealed in a duct, as with basins, and bidets are available that are cantilevered out from a wall or duct so as to leave the floor free. A soap holder and towel should be kept near at hand.

WCs

The final item of equipment is the WC and, of all the sanitary fittings, this can be the most critical in planning terms because it must be sited close to a soil pipe. Where a new bathroom is being built, or where radical alterations are being made, one is more able to site the soil pipe to suit the arrangement of the room as a whole, but altering drainage systems can be expensive. Where less fundamental changes are being made the position of an existing soil pipe will effectively control the position of the WC. Although a long, near-horizontal run of pipe is technically feasible, it is best concealed in a duct or in the floor space if it runs parallel to the joists – with access for rodding in case of a blockage, of course.

As with a bidet, the WC needs sufficient space around it for comfortable use. Sizes of WC vary and the critical dimension here is likely to be the distance from the wall to the front rim of the WC seat. At least 600mm should be added to this for access. In recent years manufacturers have been making very compact close-coupled WC suites with low-level cisterns, which eliminate the old wall-mounted cistern with its long connecting pipe and dangling chain. A flat-topped cistern can be a useful shelf in a small bathroom.

Technical details of different types of WC are given on page 64 of the reference section. The syphonic type are quieter and more efficient, but they are also more

expensive. Some cisterns are designed to be specially thin, which can be useful where space is limited or when replacing an old WC without moving the soil pipe. Other cisterns are designed for concealing in a duct and give a very neat appearance. There are types of WC that are cantilevered or corbelled out from a duct or wall to leave the floor unobstructed.

The different types of WC waste outlet – P trap, which is roughly horizontal, or S trap, which is vertical – can sometimes be ordered with right or left hand bends, which may save some space in installation.

The only accessory associated with the WC is a toilet roll holder – but it is surprising how often these are fixed in an inconvenient position.

Having considered, in general terms, how the main items of equipment in the bathroom can be used and positioned, we can go on to see how our general principles of bathroom planning work out in practice. The best way to do this is to take a selection of examples that show the problems and opportunities commonly met with. We will look in turn at a small bathroom, such as we might find in a flat or as an additional bathroom in a larger house; a bathroom of average size; and a larger than average 'luxury' bathroom. Finally, we will look at two more, rather unusual bathrooms in less conventional positions, which also demonstrate a number of interesting points about bathroom planning.

An essentially simple plan that makes extensive use of tiles to clad the walls and includes a large mirror with concealed lighting beneath it. The result is luxurious and dramatic. The purpose-built tile-clad bath is an unusual feature in this country. It does make it possible to have a bath of any size, according to choice.
Architect John Prizeman

15

Small bathroom

This is, perhaps, not quite the smallest bathroom into which we can fit the three basic fittings – basin, bath and WC – but it is near to it. It is typical, in terms of its size, of the kind of bathroom found in a small modern flat where standards of space provision are minimal, measuring 2·13 × 1·45m. It also serves to illustrate the kind of solution that may be possible where a small additional bathroom is wanted, say as part of a large main bedroom, with the least possible loss of space in the room from which it is formed. We will look at two different schemes, one a little more ambitious than the other.

The first stage is to consider the basic layout of the room. The factors that will determine the disposition of the fittings in this, and any other bathroom include not only the size of the room itself, but also its shape, the position of architectural features such as doors and windows, and whether these can be moved if they are in awkward positions.

In this example, the door is roughly in the middle of one of the long sides of the room. As the room is too short (1450mm) to place a normal length bath (1700mm) across it, the bath's position is fixed as being along the long window wall opposite the door. The position of the existing doorway then fixes the position of the basin and WC, in that the space to the left of the door is too small for the WC, which must therefore go on the right. If the WC had to be sited to the left of the door – because of the position of an existing soil pipe, for example – then it would be better to move the door about 300mm to the right.

In the case of a minimum size bathroom such as this one, the swing of the door into the room can be a nuisance. One way of getting over this problem, circumstances permitting, is to hang the door so that it opens outward. This can sometimes be done where the bathroom is *en suite* with a bedroom, or anywhere else provided that the door will not hit an unwary passer-by. Another solution is to have a sliding door. This means that there must be a free area of wall next to the door for it to slide along, and it also raises some problems of sound proofing as the result of the inevitable gap between the wall and the door.

Having established the best plan possible for the room, we can now consider the detailed planning of the room, starting with the choice of types of fittings, the arrangement of the equipment, and, finally, the accessories, finishes and decoration of the room.

Solution A

Where the budget is tight we are not likely to aim at a solution involving expensive, purpose-built fittings. A 1700mm long steel bath, with a non-slip base under the shower, is sited under the window and fitted with flexible bath/shower mixer taps. A simple ceiling-mounted shower curtain track extends 1m from the wall. A bath height boxed-in shelf at the head of the bath has some useful storage space beneath it. The side of the bath is panelled in pine boarding.

A shallow duct, also pine boarded, is built out from the basin wall to hide the pipework. This stops at a height of 900mm behind the basin to form a shelf, but it is carried up to the ceiling behind the bath. This hides the pipes to the heated towel rail mounted on it and there are small shelves for things such as bottles in the recess where it returns to the wall. A mirror is mounted on the wall above the basin, lit by a 600mm long fluorescent light fitting. An inexpensive, low-level WC suite is fitted on the opposite side of the door with a toilet roll holder on the wall adjoining. This and the other accessories are in white plastics to contrast with the varnished pine boarding. Soap holders are fitted in convenient positions for bathing and showering, and tooth mug, brush holder and facecloth hooks are fixed close to the basin.

A point to note is that the use of tongued and grooved pine boarding – fitted either vertically or horizontally – allows access panels in the same material to be easily 'lost' in the general finish. If funds permit, glazed tiles could be used on the wall behind the bath and on the return wall.

Solution B

If the budget allows it, and keeping to the same basic layout, we can be a bit more adventurous in fitting out the room and, although we cannot make space where none exists, by the careful design of some built-in fittings we can create a good deal of useful shelf and storage space – at the same time producing a scheme that 'ties up' the separate elements in the room into a unified whole. Indeed, where space is severely restricted, the kind of investment represented by this kind of thorough and detailed planning gives an even greater return for your money than if space is less limited.

By building the basin into a countertop, the amount of shelf space is increased by about three times. A cupboard below the basin fills the space between the wall and the bath and is useful for storing cleaning materials and, where there are very young children in the house, such things as the potty and nappy pail. In this case, the counter-top is surfaced in plastics laminate and has a post-formed roll front edge and coves up to a splashback behind the basin, providing a continuous and easily cleaned surface. As space is limited, a 'plug basin' – that is, a simple basin without taps or soap dish – is chosen and this is set under the countertop. Mixer taps are installed on the counter-top itself, slightly to one side as there is insufficient depth to place them centrally behind the basin. A pair of recessed soap dishes are set into the splashback to hold the soap and a nailbrush. A large mirror is mounted above the basin and, between the mirror and the right hand wall, above the end of the bath,

Solution A (right)
The small bathroom with a wall-hung basin and low-level WC suite. The bath and pipework are encased in pine boarding.

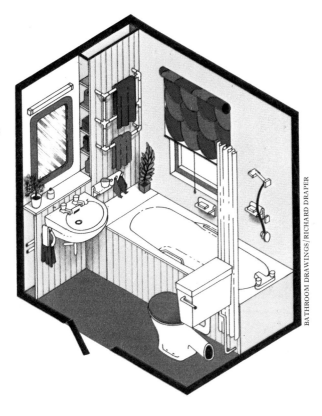

BATHROOM DRAWINGS/RICHARD DRAPER

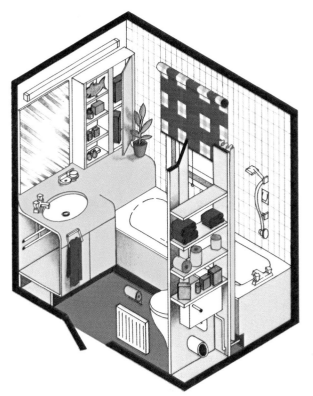

Solution B (left)
A more sophisticated arrangement with a vanitory basin set in a post-formed plastics laminate worktop and splashback. The WC cistern is concealed in a duct with a storage cupboard above it.

a special joinery fitting is formed with an enclosed section for medicines and some open shelves for toilet articles, bathtime toys, and even decorative objects. A fluorescent fitting spans almost the whole width of the wall above the mirror and fittings, giving good face and general room lighting.

The bath has independent mixer tap controls in the side wall, alongside a recessed soap dish, with the outlet at the foot of the bath. The shower has a separate thermostatic mixer valve at a convenient height and the shower head can be fitted into sockets at different heights to suit adults and children. There is also another soap recess at the right height for shower use. The walls of the bath and shower area are covered in ceramic tiles.

Shortage of storage space suggests a fitting behind the WC – space that is often wasted. The WC cistern is contained in the base of this fitting with a storage cupboard above where spare towels, toilet rolls and soap can be kept. This arrangement provides a useful feature – after all, it is in the bathroom itself that these things are needed when they run out, so it is logical to keep them there – and yet no extra space is taken up by it as it is all within the depth of the WC cistern.

Average bathroom

In this second example, we will look at an existing bathroom containing bath, basin and hot water cylinder/airing cupboard, with a separate WC. This is the kind of arrangement frequently found in small to medium-sized family houses.

When planning a bathroom of this size, the basic question is whether or not to have the WC as part of the bathroom. Generally speaking, if this is to be the only WC in the house most people will want it to be separate – except, perhaps, in the case of one or two-person households. The advantage of a separate WC is, of course, that it can be used while the bathroom is occupied. Equally, in a household where a second WC exists or is contemplated but where a single bathroom has to cater for a large family, the WC is also best kept separate. If there is relatively little pressure on the bathroom, however, there are advantages in combining the bathroom and WC spaces. The result will be a room that appears larger than the sum of the two original rooms, and also from the practical point of view, because of the bigger uninterrupted space, one with more possibilities for flexible planning. This is particularly important in the case of a bathroom, because this is where two or more of a range of possible fittings – basins, bath, shower, bidet, WC – have to be arranged in a layout that enables each one to be connected to new or existing plumbing and drainage, and be used comfortably and conveniently.

If the household is best served by having the WC separate, the existing rooms can nevertheless be improved. Should an additional fitting be wanted in the bathroom, we can create space for, say, a shower or a bidet, assuming that it is possible to site the hot water cylinder elsewhere in the house – possibly along with other improvements, such as a run of fitted wardrobes in an adjacent bedroom, or making a new utility room. By having the shower above the bath, we can, in fact,

make room for both the additional fittings. The cheapest plan for refurbishing the room then consists of retaining the bath and basin in their present positions and siting a bidet next to the end of the bath in the space formerly occupied by the hot water cylinder and airing cupboard. This is not really the best layout in the circumstances, however, because it has two definite disadvantages – both of which could be overcome by re-planning.

The first of these is that water from the shower would splash on to the window, and the second is that the position of the bidet would be somewhat awkward. A better layout is achieved by re-siting the bath across the end of the bathroom with taps and waste at the opposite end from the window. This arrangement is particularly good from the point of view of the shower, which is enclosed by adjacent walls on two sides and a screen or curtain on the third. The window wall is well away from the taps and shower and so will not be splashed. The basin and bidet are more sensibly placed side by side.

Some people might prefer to site the basin in front of the window; this is commonly done and it does have the advantage of giving splendid natural light during the daytime. The mirror does become a problem however; the only real solution is to have a mirror that swings out on an adjustable arm. This type of mirror is certainly very practical, and some of them are reversible with a magnifying shaving mirror on the back. Their chief disadvantage is one of size since, for obvious reasons, they tend to be rather small and therefore, if they are fixed at the right height for adults, not much good for children. Artificial lighting may also be difficult to provide, although if the basin is placed centrally beneath the window a pair of wall lights either side might be a satisfactory solution.

The alternative layout is to have the basin against the wall opposite the door, with the bidet between it and the bath. A simple duct built out from the wall conceals the plumbing and waste pipes for the basin and the bidet as they run under the end of the bath and out to the existing soil pipe.

Having decided where to put the fittings, we can look at what accessories and finishes will be needed to make the room work. The simplest way of providing a mirror and bathroom cabinet is to fit a proprietary bathroom cabinet on the wall above the basin. As the basin is fitted against a duct, we have the depth to do this. It is here that design problems – as opposed to planning problems – start to arise. The wall in question already has one large rectangular feature situated off centre in the form of the window. To put a ready-made cabinet over the basin will therefore add another strongly rectangular element, which will not necessarily 'read' well in juxtaposition with the window. This can be solved by a scheme of decoration that brings the cabinet, lights and shelf together in one co-ordinated design.

Solution A

In the example as shown, the cabinet has mirror-faced doors, a built-in light fitting and shaver socket. An assembly of tall cupboards, with high-level storage cupboards above, is shown beside the bath for storage of bathroom sundries, spare towels, etc. A heated towel rail is fitted near the basin and a shower curtain is hung from a ceiling track alongside the bath. A small recessed hand wash basin is provided in the separate WC. The old WC pan and high-level cistern have been replaced by a modern, low-level WC suite with a useful flat-topped cistern.

Co-ordinated fittings have been chosen and located carefully in relation to the different main sanitary fittings; tooth-brush and glass holder near the basin, and towel holder at the bidet in the bathroom; toilet roll holder, towel rail, soap holder and coat hook in the WC. Matching door handles, indicator bolts, window stays and catches complete the accessories.

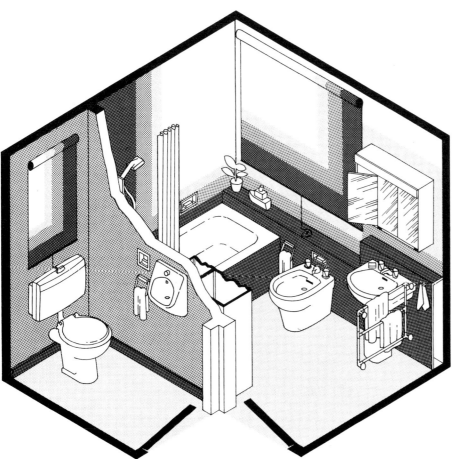

Solution B

The second plan is based on the same bathroom, but in this case the WC has been incorporated into the bathroom, which is sometimes a considerable advantage. Basin, bidet and WC are all mounted on the wall opposite the door with the bath under the window. The airing cupboard is retained in the corner of the room and contains the hot water cylinder. A shallow horizontal duct 900mm high hides all the pipework to the main fittings and provides a recessed shelf at a convenient height running the length of the bathroom.

A 1700mm long bath with flexible shower and mixer taps positioned so that they fall easily to hand provides a shower area. The ceiling track for the shower curtain extends round and past the window to protect it from splashing. The basin is wall mounted and all the fittings match, including taps, towel holders, facecloth holders and tooth mug holders. A matching bidet and close-coupled, low-level WC complete the sanitary fittings.

A special mirror is fitted above the shelf, with six tungsten lamps in simple fittings to provide light where it is most needed. Fluorescent lamps or tungsten 'architectural' tubes could be used as an alternative. The remainder of the wall is designed as a shallow wall cupboard for medicines and toiletries.

The window has a fitted roller blind, but as an alternative to this it could have a second, glazed sliding window set flush with the internal wall. If this were of obscured glass it would act as a screen from prying eyes and a protection from water from the shower, with the additional benefit of improving the thermal insulation of the room. Bath towels and bath mat can be kept on the heated towel rail fixed to the end wall above the head of the bath, the pipework to which is hidden inside the hot water cylinder cupboard.

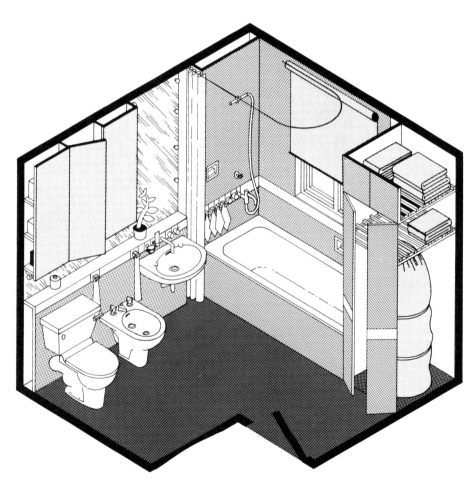

Solution C

In the third version of the bathroom, in addition to incorporating the WC into the bathroom, the hot water cylinder has been re-located in the bulkhead above the entrance area, and the airing cupboard has been moved to another part of the house. These changes allow some major improvements to be made in the planning of the room. A separate shower cubicle can be provided, made up from a standard shower tray, a partition and a curtain. The cubicle has a soap recess, a grab handle, and the shower fitting is adjustable for height. As part of the major reorganisation of the room, WC and bidet have been moved onto the return wall and a short, low partition has been built to provide partial separation. The WC cistern is hidden in a horizontal duct, which also provides a recessed 200mm wide shelf at 900mm height, which is useful for books, indoor plants, and so on, with flush-fitted cupboards above. The toilet roll holder is fixed opposite the WC on the partition. The basin and bath are arranged as in the second plan, but a counter-top basin could be fitted if preferred and would fit neatly between the partitions and the bath.

Large bathroom

In this third example, we will look at the question of how a relatively large room – 4·3 × 3·4m – can be turned into a luxurious but eminently practical bathroom suitable for a well heeled couple without children, or a family who have the use of another bathroom. The room might be an unwanted extra bedroom, for example.

This is a room of ample size, and this means that the opportunity can be taken to plan a room that is almost a living/bathroom – with a seating area as well as the more usual bath, shower, twin basins, bidet and WC. The bath is recessed in a specially constructed tiled plinth and surround, which provides a generous amount of space for putting books, clothes or drinks on. Cushions can be put on the step for sitting on, and it also facilitates entry to the bath itself.

The shower cubicle is also purpose-built, and incorporates a seat, soap recess and grab handle. A glass door stops surplus water from spilling into the room and the cubicle is artificially ventilated through a grille leading to a duct in the ceiling space above in which an extractor fan is fitted. This also ventilates the room.

The twin wash basins, which could be either circular or oval, are built into a tiled counter. This is made from a blockboard top and front mounted on a specially designed cupboard unit with faced hinged doors, which also provide access to the plumbing. The tiles used are 150 × 75mm throughout. The counter itself has recessed plant pots built into it and, above the basins, well lit mirrors are mounted out from the wall on framing and a fluorescent tube fitted behind them to give indirect light to the counter. Separate lights at head height illuminate the face.

The WC and bidet are corbel type fittings which leave the floor free from obstructions. The wall on which they are mounted is a complete storage wall with cupboards and space for the concealed WC cistern. The cupboards, which are 200mm deep, are useful for storing medicines and toilet items.

The seating in the room is made up from thick, cushioned seats and backs covered in washable fabric, and there are wall lights above this area. The floor is close carpeted and the window has a matching blind. A low coffee table completes the furnishings. Towels for the bath and shower are kept on a heated towel rail at the head of the bath and, for washing, two towel rings are provided, one to the left of each basin.

All in all, this is a room with a number of interesting features and it would be a good place in which to relax or get away from the rest of the family while having a luxurious soak.

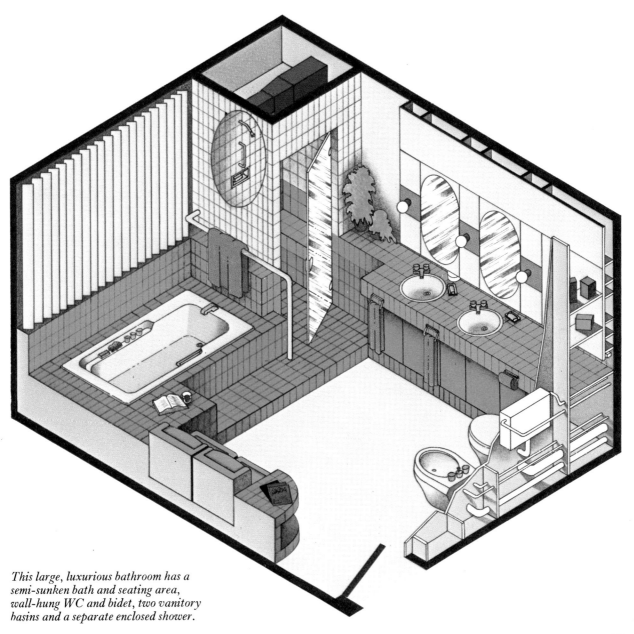

This large, luxurious bathroom has a semi-sunken bath and seating area, wall-hung WC and bidet, two vanitory basins and a separate enclosed shower.

Two unusual bathrooms

The last two examples in this section show unusual solutions to design problems posed by the need to install new bathrooms in existing houses. In the first, the solution was to provide a circular bathroom in the centre of the top floor of an early Victorian town house; in the second, a very small bathroom was fitted into the space above the staircase of a Georgian house in London. Both these schemes show how an imaginative solution can produce sometimes unforeseen advantages, as well as solving apparently impossible problems.

The circular bathroom shows how the maximum benefit can be gained by using existing space in an imaginative way. The top floor of an old house was converted to provide a children's room with three beds, together with a separate bedroom for visitors. The circular bathroom, which is lit from above, was fitted into the centre of the space and it contains a bath, shower, WC and counter-top basin. The shapes left over after these items had been installed provide very practical shelf space and seating, allowing foot-washing and showering among other things. Mosaic tiles were used throughout – white on the walls and dark blue for the steps, shelves and seat. In this case, a radical approach to planning the whole floor space has solved several problems at once and, in addition, an aesthetically satisfying result emerges through the contrast of colour and form.

In the case of the bathroom fitted into the roof space of a Georgian house, there was just enough room over the top of the staircase in the upper part of the house to insert a very small, but practical, bathroom containing a bath, basin and WC. The additional six steps up to the bathroom provided sufficient headroom below it and a satisfactory head of water was ensured by installing the cold water tank in the bulkhead over the new stairs. The bath has corner-mounted taps and a storage cupboard is built into the space at its foot. The basin is mounted on a shallow duct wall incorporating all the pipework as well as a wall cabinet and mirror. A shelf runs the full length of the room below the cabinet.

A top-lit, internal bathroom using standard basin, bath and WC set in mosaic tiled surfaces which also form a purpose-built shower.

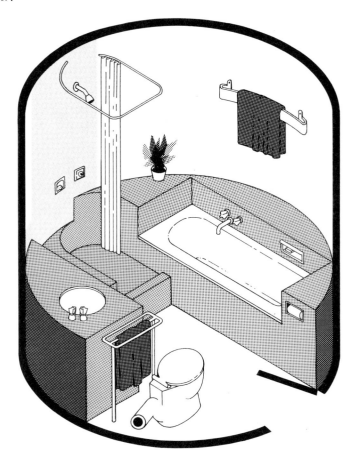

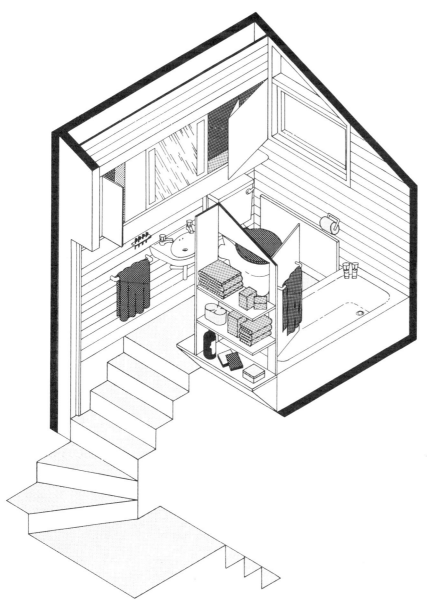

A near-minimum bathroom inserted in a roof space above a flight of stairs. The specially designed cupboard fitting also incorporates a shutter for the window.

An ABC of bathrooms

Accessories

Bathroom accessories include items such as towel rails, soap holders, toothbrush racks, hooks, toilet roll holders and so on. Towel rails are dealt with under their own heading on page 56, as many of them do not form part of an accessory range.

Matching ranges of accessories are available in a variety of designs, materials and finishes, including metal, ceramics and plastics. Having as many of the accessories in a bathroom as possible matching one another adds to the thought-out look of the room and helps to impose an overall stamp on it. The actual design of the accessories you choose will only affect the character of the room in detail, but it is in the detail that a concept is made or marred. Some designs are made in ranges to match other elements of the bathroom, such as ironmongery, taps, or wall finishes. The design of your bathroom and its finishes will help to indicate the most suitable choice, but you should remember to pick accessories that work well in addition to looking good – it is important that they should be easily cleaned, for example.

The most common finish for accessories has in the past been chromium plate, and this is possibly still the case. This finish has the advantage of matching taps, most of which are also chromium plated. It is a thoroughly tried and tested finish and good quality chrome stands up well to the kind of use and atmosphere usually found in a bathroom. The items available cover all requirements, including towel rails and rings, hooks for facecloths and bath-robes, toothbrush and tooth glass holders, toilet roll and pack holders, soap dishes and magnetic soap holders, shelf supports, ashtrays, and so on. The more sophisticated ranges have concealed fixings, which look particularly neat. There are many makes on the market and builders' merchants, hardware shops and department stores generally have one or more ranges to choose from.

Ceramic bathroom accessories have long been familiar. They are made by tile manufacturers in sizes and colours to fit in with and match tiled walls. Again, items are available to satisfy every need. Many designs have been around for some time and may, perhaps, not represent the latest thoughts in product design. Even so, where a bathroom is being partially or wholly tiled they are a very neat way of providing accessories, since they fit into the tile module and form an integral part of the wall. This gives them a purposeful, built-in look which is less easy to achieve with surface-mounted accessories. They are also the only simple way of providing recessed holders for soap, sponges and nailbrushes, thus minimising obtrusions and preserving the flush finish of a wall. It is worth noting that ceramic accessories can be used in conjunction with mosaic wall finishes by choosing an appropriate colour.

DAVID CRIPPS

There are some complete architectural ranges that include bathroom accessories and offer a comprehensive selection of fittings for the rest of the house. Thus the bathroom accessories can match the door and window furniture in the bathroom, including knobs, handles, bolts and catches, and can even match other ironmongery throughout the house, including electrical accessories in some cases.

A relatively recent development in bathroom fittings has been the introduction of coloured finishes, such as epoxy resin, for metal equipment. This has enabled ranges to be offered in bright, co-ordinated colours with matching taps, controls and accessories. Developments in plastics have meant that fittings such as taps can be produced from these materials in colours to match accessories and sanitary equipment in the bathroom. Brass, bronze and gold plated fittings are also made in a variety of designs, including traditional and fanciful patterns for use where these are appropriate – but remember that function comes first.

Good quality plastics are suitable materials for forming complex shapes and a number of accessory ranges are made from these materials. The results are happier in some cases than in others. Visual appearance is, of course, a matter of personal taste; whether an accessory does the job it is intended to do is not. A towel ring, for example, that is too springy and comes out of its bracket in use is a practical failure, and it is a sad fact that by no means all products on the market are well suited to the purpose for which they are intended.

Siting accessories is dealt with in some detail in the section on bathroom planning and in the worked-through examples. Suffice it to say here that, when arranging accessories, you should give careful thought to their position relative to the fittings with which they will be used. There is no better way of doing this than 'going through the motions' – by standing at the basin, for example, and reaching

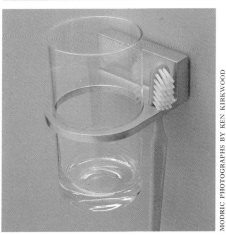

Left: fittings from the Allgood Modric range in silver anodised aluminium. From top, toilet roll holder, soap dish, magnetic soap-holder, toothbrush and tumbler holder. Other items in the range are shown on page 45. Below: part of the Crayonne bathroom range in polished ABS plastics.

MODRIC PHOTOGRAPHS BY KEN KIRKWOOD

for a toothbrush or towel, or standing in the shower and reaching for the controls and the soap dish. You should not assume that the conventional positions, or those that you have lived with before, are necessarily the best ones for you, although they may provide something to start from (why, for example, are light switches often placed so high?) and where several members of a family share a bathroom, the positions will necessarily be a compromise. Some useful heights are given in the section on shapes and sizes on pages 53–54.

Airing cupboards

Airing cupboards are frequently associated with the bathroom. There is no particular advantage in this arrangement from the planning point of view, nor for the user. An airing cupboard, adequately heated and ventilated, is an essential part of a well run home, however, and should on no account be reduced to a low priority when considering the bathroom. The cupboard can be heated either by a radiator connected to the domestic hot water circuit, or by one connected to the central heating circuit with a summer auxiliary heater. Small electric airing cupboard heaters of about 80 watt capacity can be effective if properly located. Waste heat from the refrigerator or freezer could usefully be saved and used to heat the airing cupboard, but this would require ingenuity and forethought. Whether it is a good idea to use the hot water cylinder itself to heat the cupboard is arguable. If the cylinder is lagged to the latest requirements of the Building Regulations, with 75mm of fibreglass quilt or its equivalent, it seems pointless to then open up one section to allow heat into the airing cupboard.

The best shelving in an airing cupboard is still simple slatted untreated softwood 50 × 25mm. This is comparatively cheap and a choice of supports can be provided.

Architects and designers

An architect experienced in domestic work or a properly trained interior designer is of course the person best able to design your bathroom.

A bathroom is but a microcosm of the problems of those engaged in designing for habitations. There are about 3500 private architectural practices and over 2000 design practices in this country. The Design Council's Designer Selection Service, the RIBA Clients' Advisory Bureau, and the SIAD Designers' Information Service all have well documented registers of architects and designers. It is important that you should choose an individual or firm experienced in and willing to undertake this sort of work and these organisations, whose addresses and telephone numbers are listed at the end of this book, will give you names of suitable architects and designers in your area. There are standard fee scales for work undertaken, and you can rely on the integrity of your professional adviser to look after your interests. Should you decide to go ahead on your own, unless you are a do-it-yourself expert of a high order, remember that you are acting the part of the professional and will inevitably become embroiled in all the day-to-day frustrations and irritations he is used to. In choosing fittings for example, on the face of it a simple enough task, it may be interesting to note that the list of manufacturers and their addresses and products appearing on pages 69–70, took over five days of full time work to assemble.

Remember also that, in the event of your employing outside labour to carry out the work, you will be in the hands of the builder or his tradesmen. You will be told that things cannot be done which you want done, or that something must be done in a particular way and that way only. Such assertions may be true, but they may only be made to make life easier for whoever is doing the work. On cost also, you will be on your own with no way

of arguing on the validity of any items charged. If money is no object, many firms of specialist bathroom installers will be ready to help you spend your money. Such things as gold plated bath and shower fittings will cost you anything up to £150 per set; a well designed chrome plated set, on the other hand, may be found for approximately £25.

Asiatic closets

These are also referred to as Continental closets and are familiar features of the sanitary arrangements found in the Middle East. Most readers of this book will no doubt be as mystified as the authors as to how such a monstrous design was ever arrived at. There are, nevertheless, certain health advantages to counterbalance the obvious disadvantages and embarrassments provided by this fitting. The squatting position is probably medically better than the nearly level seat of the ordinary water closet. There has been a certain amount of argument on this in recent years and it is possible to obtain a 'half way' compromise closet, should this be desired. If an Asiatic closet is to be provided this cannot be in the bathroom. Certain design features in the room in which this is to be fitted would greatly ease the difficulties experienced by Western users. These include careful design of the floor itself, and hooks for hanging clothes.

Basins

During the past few years manufacturers have drastically reduced the number of different designs of basin available. This has reduced the problem of choosing a single basin from a vast range, but it has made it more difficult to find the right basin for a particular purpose.

The materials used for basins include vitreous china, glazed earthenware, glazed

Pedestal basins

These allow pipework to be largely concealed provided that care is taken with the plumbing.

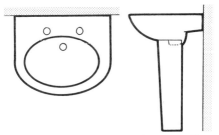

Ideal-Standard Brasilia. Water supplies and waste taken through wall at high level, just below basin.

Wall-hung basins

Many sizes and shapes are available. Most, but not all, have holes to suit mixer taps.

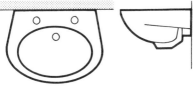

Armitage Shanks Rose. Good clearance behind bowl gives space for face and hair washing. Flat 'put-down' areas.

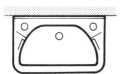

Ideal-Standard. Shallow basin for use in WCs etc.

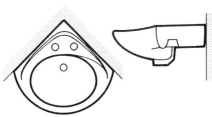

Ideal-Standard Angle. For corner fixing in small bathrooms and WCs where space is at a premium.

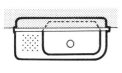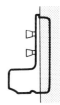

Twyfords Barbican. Recessed into the wall and useful where space is very limited. Plumbing must be carried into the wall.

Countertop basins

Many designs available. Those that fit below a hole cut in a countertop look more elegant and avoid raised lips, but need skill to fit.

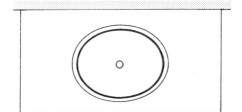

Armitage Shanks Seville. One-piece ceramic construction avoids jointing problems, but maximum length limited.

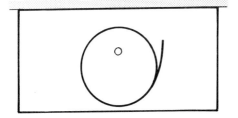

Armitage Shanks Marlow. Fitted under countertop and needs good workmanship.

fireclay, plastics, stainless steel and pressed steel with a vitreous enamel coating. Vitreous china is the most common material. For a discussion of the different characteristics of these materials see page 48.

Basins can be cantilevered out from the wall on brackets or supported on legs from the floor and pedestals are available which are intended to hide the pipework. It is becoming increasingly popular to choose basins that can be fitted into a counter-top or vanitory unit. Some of these are relatively easily fitted, with a lip that covers any gap between the basin and its surround; others require more skilful fitting and finishing of the counter-top. Inspecting manufacturers' catalogues or the basin itself will give you a good idea of how difficult the job is likely to be.

In any case, the most important detail consideration is probably the layout of the supply and waste pipework. Most people would agree that exposed pipework tends to be ugly and the general practice is to conceal it in some form of ducting, which must be designed to provide access for maintenance purposes. Ducts can take the form of complete hollow walls behind the basin, or a hollow wall up to a short distance above it, in which case the ledge can be used as a shelf. Pedestal basins conceal the pipework to some extent, but often incompletely, and may require quite skilful plumbing to achieve even this.

Basins must obviously be chosen to be sufficiently large for the job they have to do. It is usually difficult to imagine how a basin will perform when installed from its appearance in a catalogue or a showroom, but there are some points to look out for. In the first place, the basin must be sufficiently wide and deep from back to front to enable hands, face and hair to be washed without water dripping onto the floor in front and without bumping one's head on the wall behind. It must also be deep enough from top to bottom; a basin with curving sides and a

deep centre will fill up more quickly initially and thus save some water. There should, of course, be a place for the soap that will actually retain the soap while allowing excess water to drain away – it is surprising how many basins let the soap slide gently into the water just as one is rinsing off. Places are also needed for nail brushes and other items and a basin with plenty of flat surfaces is a boon. Manufacturers seem to be realising the advantages which these offer over 'sculptured' surfaces of doubtful beauty and little practical value. Few basins, however, have all the flat surface that is needed and it is usually necessary to have shelves or counter-tops close to the basin in addition.

Basins are normally provided with tap holes, although not all of them are spaced so that a mixer tap can be fitted and mixer taps are useful for quick hand-washing. For wall or duct-mounted taps the basin will have to be one without holes and a good number of designs are available in this form. It may be an advantage to have separate taps widely spaced, so that they are not in the way when washing one's hair, for example. In very confined spaces, corner-mounted basins can be useful, but they are generally a good deal smaller than the average; they may be big enough for adding to a separate WC however.

As with all the other major pieces of bathroom equipment, basins are available in a number of colours; recent trends have been towards stronger and brighter hues. You should, however, ask yourself whether choosing a matching set of coloured bath, basin, WC, and possibly shower and bidet will be worth the extra cost, or whether the money might be better spent. White china fittings are clean and smart, and allow any choice of wall, floor and ceiling finishes.

Baths

Baths are available in a multitude of shapes and sizes, and in a number of different materials and colours. They can be made of glazed fireclay, vitreous enamelled pressed sheet steel, porcelain enamelled cast iron, acrylic plastics, or glass fibre reinforced plastics (GRP). These materials are discussed in more detail on page 48. They all have their advantages and disadvantages, but on balance and given reasonable precautions in installation, use and cleaning, all these materials are quite satisfactory. It is probably best to choose a bath that suits your needs from all the other points of view and then worry about what material it is made of.

The average size for baths in this country is 1700mm long and about 700mm wide. Shorter baths than this are available,

Twyfords Curran Standard. Typical of the sort of basic bath available in a range of sizes and made of porcelain-enamelled cast-iron, pressed steel and plastics.

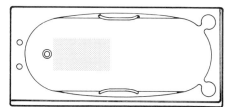

Ideal-Standard New Status. Luxury bath with built-in soap recesses, handgrips and a slip-resistant area for showering.

but they are less satisfactory in use and should only be installed where space is severely restricted. Most baths can be fitted in several positions relative to walls or partitions in the bathroom – with one side, a side and an end, or a side and both ends against a wall for example. Most manufacturers supply side panels to suit these different arrangements, but you may prefer to have a purpose-built panel to suit the materials in the rest of your bathroom.

Holes for taps are also provided in various positions to suit different installations. The most usual arrangement is to have taps and waste grouped at one end of the bath, but taps at one corner may be more convenient in some cases and taps and waste placed centrally in one side of the bath can be a good idea if you're in the habit of sharing.

More expensive baths often have some extra features, including non-slip showering areas, built-in soap holders and grab handles. These are all well worth having but some expensive baths seem to vie with each other in bad taste.

Among the more unusual baths are those designed to fit diagonally across a corner of the bathroom, where space allows, circular baths and so on. Sunken baths can be provided, at a price, by excavating a hole in a ground floor bathroom, or by building up a surrounding plinth.

In terms of colour, as with other fittings, the simplest choice may be the best in the long run. Fashionable colours come and go, and it is a mistake to spend a lot of money on an up-to-the-minute colour for expensive fittings such as baths, basins and WCs only to find that your tastes change and redecoration in keeping with these major items is difficult.

Left: Vogue Elysian. Generous, sensibly shaped bath in cast iron with side taps and foot spout, built-in handgrips and integral soap recesses.
Below: This Oriental soaking tub, by Ideal Standard, is based on a traditional Japanese design. It combines a shower and a sit-down bath in little more space than is taken up by a conventional shower.

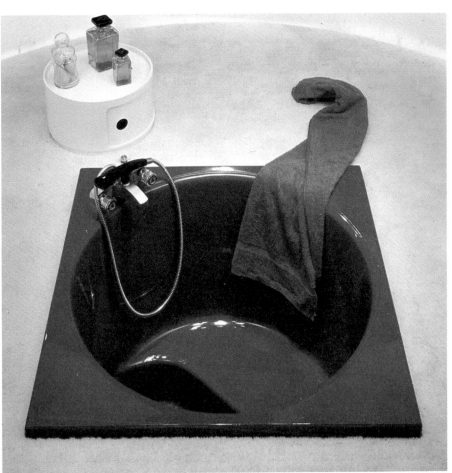

Twyfords Caravelle. Simple bidet with 'over rim' water supply from inexpensive pillar taps.

Ideal-Standard Brasilia. Flushing rim bidet with ascending spray and pop-up waste.

Armitage Shanks Braemar. Wall-hung design fits tightly against the wall and leaves the floor clear.

Armitage Shanks Profile. Bidet with over rim water supply designed for duct mounting with wall-mounted mixer tap.

Bidets

Although they are now becoming more popular in this country, bidets in the past were only known to intrepid Continental travellers as objects of mystery and imagination. Were they for washing feet? Why were the French so particular about their feet? Later it dawned that there were more 'adult' uses.

The fitting is, of course, complementary to the hand wash basin, which is useful for washing down to waist level but rather clumsy below that. A bidet only needs a waste pipe similar to that for a basin (30mm) and hot and cold water supply. It takes up a comparatively small amount of space and is a useful extra. Most manufacturers make bidets to match basins and WCs.

The simplest form of bidet consists of a low, floor-standing pedestal with hot and cold taps discharging into the bowl, which has a waste plug and chain. More sophisticated models have a flushing rim arrangement similar to that of a WC pan whereby water is discharged behind a turned down lip running around the top of the basin. This has the advantage of warming the rim (on which one sits) and rinsing the whole bowl after use. This type often has a 'pop-up' waste controlled from between the taps instead of a plug and chain. Some bidets have the added refinement of a douche or ascending spray, rather like an inverted shower, to which the incoming water can be diverted. It is worth checking with your local authority before ordering a bidet. Most water boards have special requirements for the installation of bidets with a douche attachment aimed at preventing back syphonage and contamination of the water supply when the spray is immersed in dirty water.

Builders

It is a common complaint of architects and designers that people go straight to a builder to get their houses built or altered. On the face of it, this complaint seems unworthy of the profession and yet another example of the conspiracy against the laity. Nevertheless, builders are in business to build, and not to design buildings, and designers are in business to design and see their designs are properly carried out by the specialists in building. Given a good working relationship, this arrangement is best. If you decide to design your own bathroom, then you are taking on the role of the architect or designer, and you should not rely on the builder for this aspect of the project. Some builders, of course, will try to carry out the designer's function, but since the motivation of the builder is different from that of the designer, many compromises on design are likely to result.

A good builder, on the other hand, is essential for successfully carrying out a bathroom project. The owner may wish to employ tradesmen such as plumbers, drain-layers, carpenters and electricians, direct, but let him be warned, because he will inevitably find himself doing the builder's job of co-ordinating, ordering materials, chasing up tradesmen and all the other activities that fill a professional builder's working hours. It can be done, but the experience is likely to be painful, and will inevitably take longer than it would with a well organised builder. Choosing a builder is always difficult. This is still an old-fashioned industry, but old-established, small builders know what it is all about. Go and see as many builders in their offices as you can. Glossy offices can be misleading, but beware the small man with no apparent administrative back-up at all. This usually spells disaster. Obtain personal recommendations from other people in the area who have undertaken the same work. Time spent on choosing a builder is time well spent.

Builders' merchants

A builders' merchant will be found in any sizeable town. The average builders' merchant will be able to supply nearly anything that is currently available, but not necessarily out of his stock. Generally, a restricted range of proprietary products is available over the counter, and standard builders' and plumbers' materials are of course always to be got. However, special proprietary items are a very different matter. Imported goods may be difficult to get through your local merchant but, more important, unusual items are often on extended delivery. Some manufacturers wait until they have sufficient orders for, say, a special spray tap, before actually producing any at all, and the delivery period may extend to six months or more. Many manufacturers will only supply through a merchant and you should check this at the time of choosing. It is important, therefore, to establish a friendly relationship with your local merchant, who will be able to arrange a monthly account on receipt of suitable references. If the work is being done without a builder, this arrangement will probably prove indispensable.

Building regulations

Building regulations are laid down by the Department of the Environment and are administered and enforced by local district councils. They apply in England and Wales, excluding the old London County Council Area, which comes under the London Building Acts. In Scotland the Scottish Building Regulations apply. All new, permanent, domestic buildings must comply with whichever regulations cover the locality involved. Alterations to buildings must also comply. Broadly speaking, as far as bathrooms are concerned the regulations that apply are Parts A, B, C, D, F, K, N and P, although some paragraphs in other sections must be noted. In practice, if you have no professional advice at hand it is sensible to visit your local District Council Building Inspector and establish friendly relations with him; frequently these people can be helpful, but if treated wrongly can make your life a misery. They are usually best seen early in the day, before they leave for site visits. Your friendly, local building inspector will certainly know the Building Regulations – they are his Bible. Unfortunately, they are written in the form of English, beloved of Parliamentary draftsmen and lawyers, that ensures that the meaning is obscure to the ordinary, well educated citizen. This results in moments of near hysteria when attempting to distil the significant meaning from a paragraph such as this:

'**3** If such room has one window only, there shall be a minimum zone of open space outside the window such as to leave adjacent to the window an upright shaft of space wholly open to the sky (with the exception of any projection permitted by paragraph 6), the base of the shaft being formed by a plane inclined upwards at an angle of 30 degrees to the horizontal from the wall at the lower window level and its sides coinciding with the following four vertical planes:

(a) an outer plane which is parallel to the wall and which –
(i) is at a distance from the wall of 12 feet, or such a distance as may be required by paragraph 7 of this regulation, or (subject to a limit of 50 feet) one half the distance between the upper window level and the top of the wall containing the window, whichever is greatest; and
(ii) has a width equal to its required distance from the wall; and
(iii) is so located that some part of it is directly opposite some part of the window; and
(b) an inner plane which coincides with the external surface of the wall and which:

(i) has a width such that the product of that width and the window height equals one tenth of the floor area of the room containing the window; and

(ii) is located wholly between the sides of the window or, where it is required to be wider than the window, is so located that it extends across the whole width of the window, and overlaps it on either or both sides; and

(c) two lateral planes joining the corresponding extremities of the inner plane and outer plane.'

This should confirm the advice that your best friend will be your local council official. In Inner London the situation is even more complicated: London Building Acts and London Building Bye-laws apply and enforcement is by district surveyor for structural matters and London Borough Council for sanitation and drainage. It should not be assumed that these regulations are in any way unnecessary; their origins lie in the early Public Health Acts, the introduction of which was an essential move in the improvement of conditions in the last century. They embody principles of good practice that ought to be followed, whether or not the regulations exist.

Cabinets

It is only fairly recently that much thought seems to have gone into the design of proprietary bathroom cabinets. We are all familiar with the old metal cabinet with a mirror on the door and strange little metal catches. Nowadays, however, melamine-faced wooden cabinets are readily available and, with the development of plastics, there are a number of good bathroom cabinets on the market made from these materials. Some of these incorporate such refinements as fluorescent strip-lighting above the mirror, doors, electric shaver sockets, thermo-

meters, and fitted racks inside doors for toothbrushes and other small items. Where there are young children in the house and medicines are kept in the bathroom cabinet (not necessarily the best place for them, by the way) then it is essential that there should be a good lock on the cabinet door. There are a number of specially designed medicine cabinets on the market that a young child will find it impossible to open.

Recently some manufacturers have turned their attention to producing ranges of wall storage cupboards for the bathroom, incorporating drawers, cupboards, counter-tops with inset basins, shelves and mirror-fronted cabinets. This means that it is possible to fit out one or more walls of a bathroom with a 'storage wall' assembly – the kitchen fitting-out approach applied to the bathroom, in fact – which will provide space for everything likely to be needed.

It is frequently possible, on a smaller scale, to incorporate storage for small items into the design of the bathroom as a whole. For example, a wall designed to conceal the WC cistern can provide a shallow cupboard for medicines and bathroom supplies. It can be constructed of birch-faced plywood and lacquered or stained, or melamine-faced board, or painted blockboard. Varnished pine boarding is extremely versatile and can be used for wall panelling and concealed cupboard doors.

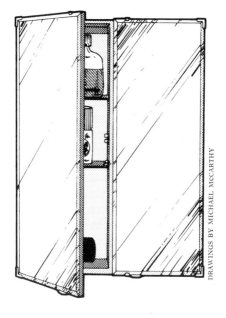

DRAWINGS BY MICHAEL MCCARTHY

*Right: A useful detail of the bathroom
shown on page 57 is the storage cupboard
and mirror built into the often wasted space
above the WC cistern, which it hides.
Designer Nicholas Hills*

*Opposite and above: Some proprietary
solutions to bathroom storage. Top left is a
Metlex double door cabinet with mirror
doors, available in a range of sizes. Below it
is an Allibert Fascination cabinet with
central shelf and mirror, strip lighting and
side cupboards with mirror doors. An open
plastics unit like the one above holds quite a
lot and adds a touch of colour in the
process.*

*Simple white fittings, painted brickwork
and timber boarding in a sophisticated but
practical scheme. The wide shelf around the
bath gives lots of space for bottles and bathtime toys, and towels are kept dry by the
warm air duct recessed in the bath panel.
Architect Peter Aldington*

RICHARD EINZIG

Carpets

A luxury bathroom in our climate nowadays usually means having a fitted carpet, but carpets are of course affected by water. If a bathroom that gets heavy family use with splashing is to be carpeted, care must be taken in the choice of carpet material. Synthetic fibres – such as nylon or acrylic – do not absorb moisture as do natural fibres. Thus a carpet with a synthetic pile and natural backing will allow the moisture to run through to the backing where it cannot easily evaporate, and so the carpet will eventually deteriorate and rot. The backing as well as the pile should therefore be synthetic. Some acrylic fibres tend to matt down, or 'felt', when wet and are less suitable than others. Rubber backed carpets are particularly suitable as they prevent moisture from reaching the floor and being trapped between it and the carpet. Rubber backed carpet tiles are a possibility and can be moved around. Those where the joints are not emphasised are better in small areas such as bathrooms – particularly as the floor space may have odd shapes cut out of it in the form of WC pan and bidet, pedestal basin, etc. Natural fibres, such as wool, are better used where a bathroom is likely to have careful adult users and where there is central heating.

Choice of colour and pattern is a matter of interior decoration, but generally lighter colours are preferable in small areas and these do not show up talc, lint, etc, as do dark colours. Where a bathroom is to be carpeted and is *en suite* with a bedroom, the carpet in each room should be the same.

Ceilings

In existing houses the ceiling will probably be plasterboard or plaster on laths. As far as bathrooms are concerned, there are a number of alternative ceiling materials that are suitable, as well as a considerable choice of finishes. Varnished or stained timber boarding lasts extremely well in bathroom conditions. In bathrooms with condensation problems polystyrene tiles should be considered. This material has a warm surface that copes well with moisture and remains clean and fresh-looking for a surprisingly long time. They can be obtained from do-it-yourself shops and fixed with special adhesive. An alternative would be to use acoustic tiles, possibly to provide a false ceiling in which lights and ventilation can be recessed, but it is important to check that the tiles are intended for use in damp or steamy places.

Plastered ceilings require decoration and any good quality paint should prove satisfactory. Anti-condensation paints are available with a gritty texture, but usually there is a poor choice of colours.

Children

Bathrooms have to cater for all the seven ages of man, and this leads to some of the problems associated with use of the room. The conventional bath is too low down for anyone easily to bath a young child; the basin is too high for a child to use; the taps are too stiff; the water is too hot; the shower is too high and so on. Attempts to provide special fixtures simply transfer the problem to the next size up. However, as with the elderly and the disabled, a few design features can easily be incorporated and the sensible use of furniture can help. An easily movable seat such as a small stool that can be used for sitting on when bathing young children is a boon. If the WC is sited close to the bath, the cover of this makes a good seat to use for this purpose. Grab handles by the bath, non-slip surfaces and good storage space for boats, ducks, etc, will help to make the bathroom usable by others, but if a children's bathroom is specifically required, certain advantages result. The smallest size of bath (1370mm) can be used, thus dramatically reducing the space required. In fact, a children's bathroom with bath, WC and basin, can be fitted into a space 1320mm by 1675mm. Such an arrangement might be well worth considering.

Hilary Gelson's book on *Children about the house* in this series contains a number of useful tips on adapting a bathroom to children's needs and on safety.

Colour

Architects and designers deal with colour in a different way from the untrained layman. They consider colour as only one aspect of a material, texture being the other. It is best always to think, like them, in terms of texture and colour – and of course in terms of lighting, since daylight and artificial light produce different effects on the same material. Consider whether your room is used mainly in daytime or at night; many rooms that seem stimulating and satisfying by artificial light look tawdry in the cold light of day. Your bathroom has to do duty in both situations; try and take advantage of the good qualities of both daylight and artificial light. If your bathroom window faces east or south-east, take advantage of the early sunlight and plan your colours with this in mind.

Most 'luxury' bathrooms illustrated in books and magazines exist only in the showroom or the photographer's studio and give a false impression of what can be achieved. The majority of bathrooms are comparatively small, and contain a good deal of clutter; toothbrushes, mirrors, towels and so on contribute to the visual scene in both a positive and a negative way. Your bathroom is primarily a functional room but it should satisfy your visual sense when in use. Colour is an inducer of mood; if your preference is for a feeling of healthy, Nordic cleanliness, then your bathroom will probably contain no applied colour at all; natural timber, white plaster, white fittings, coloured towels and so on may well be the best solution. If, however, you see your bathroom as a background to your fantasy life then anything is permissible. One thing that can be said: make your bathroom a genuine expression of your personality, and not of some advertiser's vision of luxury living. Colour changes in walls and floors are easy to achieve; experimentation in colour is probably best carried out in the bathroom. As far as paint colours are concerned, obtain the latest British Standard 4800 colour range which is quite good for most colours. It has weaknesses, but it probably gives a wider range than your local do-it-yourself merchant will stock. Look also at coloured timber stains and think about the use of natural timber or birch-faced plywood. Be careful when choosing coloured tiles and look at tiles *in situ*. Finally, always consider your lighting arrangements at the same time; coloured light bulbs and dimmer switches can produce results as interesting as the applied colours themselves.

Coloured fittings in a bathroom are a matter of personal taste – and tastes change, so you should think carefully about installing expensive coloured fittings which may go out of fashion. On a practical note, however, fittings from different manufacturers and in different materials can show slight variations in colour. For a perfect match it is best to make a careful comparison in the showroom or builders' merchant's store.

Left: A simple bathroom in a modern house. The architecture determines the character of the room, with white painted brickwork and varnished pine boarding. Colour is provided by two elements – the blue plastics splashback behind the basin and the bright red WC seat. Architect Peter Aldington

Below left: A simple basic arrangement in this bathroom, with highly personalised decorations.
Below right: The bold use of a single strong colour in combination with plain, simple finishes gives this bathroom a very personal appeal at reasonable cost.

Condensation

Condensation has become a bugbear of modern living. It results from our methods of building, our methods of heating and our social habits, and it can only be dealt with by intelligent design and living habits. As everyone knows, the bathroom is probably one of the most vulnerable rooms in the house. In the old-fashioned bathroom condensation did not matter very much, but as soon as more 'luxurious' arrangements are provided, trouble is likely. For example, the incorporation of a dressing area with clothes storage can lead, at the worst, to damp, mouldy conditions in the hanging space due to cold wall surfaces and lack of ventilation. Warm-air heating systems frequently do not help the problem, particularly with draught excluders on doors and windows and no open fireplaces.

As far as the bathroom is concerned it is advisable to have some permanent background heat, very good ventilation, and surfaces and materials that do not suffer from intermittent moisture.

Emulsion paint, wallpaper, some curtain fabrics and carpets deteriorate with excessive condensation, while tiles, mosaic, treated timber, gloss paint and vinyl wall coverings are all fairly robust in this context. An extractor fan can be invaluable under extreme conditions, but remember that domestic fans are frequently noisy in use and can be extremely irritating.

Curtains and blinds

The choice of fabric designs for use in the bathroom is beyond the scope of this book, but the question of curtain track needs consideration. If conventional curtains are to be used there is a considerable choice of track. Many shops stock only a few types, but it is possible to find, for example, very neat aluminium track that can be left exposed and looks good without a pelmet. Others can be let in flush with the ceiling, which is easier if a new ceiling is being installed and its construction can be designed with this in mind. Curtain track fitted in this way is virtually invisible.

Although soft furnishings are likely to deteriorate more rapidly in a bathroom than in other rooms, good ventilation can go some way towards mitigating this problem. An extractor fan, if properly installed, will get rid of steam, but not immediately – and in any case you must remember to switch it on. As far as curtain fabrics are concerned, most cotton prints are satisfactory, although close weave fabrics are preferable because shrinkage is reduced. A resin impregnated finish or an 'easycare' fabric is better still, and a similar finish can be applied in aerosol form. Man-made fibres, such as acrylics and glass fibre, are also satisfactory as they are non-absorbent, although some are a little flimsy. Should you wish to use a decorative fabric as a shower curtain, it is possible to attach a waterproof plastics lining to the inside face.

If your bathroom windows are of handsome Georgian proportions, it is as well to follow the example of the Georgians themselves and forego curtains. In this case, simple roller blinds are both economical and appropriate. Laminated fabric for blinds is more durable for bathroom use. Other types of blinds include Venetian, the traditional pinoleum roller blinds, and vertical louvre blinds with either plastics or fabric louvres. The last type are well worth considering for a bathroom as they give a sophisticated appearance and are easy to operate.

Design of fittings

The design of bathroom fittings is something that is largely a matter of personal preference. The Design Centres and Design Index provide information on ranges of well designed fittings and accessories, and if you study manufacturers' lists and advertisements you will probably find yourself well able to pick out good examples of product design as opposed to bad ones. It is important, though, to distinguish between styling, which is imposed on a product late in its development, and true design, which takes all the different factors of performance, safety, construction, ergonomics, aesthetics and cost into account. A really well designed piece of bathroom equipment will do its job properly, safely and easily, and be made of appropriate materials in a form that is visually pleasing and practical.

A well designed product should also provide good value for money and this is where some problems may arise. There has been a tendency over the past decade for manufacturers to concentrate on the concept of luxury in bathroom fittings and the advertisers have had a great time in selling this idea to consumers like ourselves. Unfortunately this approach does not, in itself, lead to well designed products or well planned bathrooms. Picking a richly coloured oval bath with matching basins, WC and bidet, together with gold-plated taps and fittings, could easily cost well over £600, and more out-of-the-way choices could push the price much higher still. Mosaic wall coverings, thick pile carpets and plenty of accessories can add hundreds of pounds to the bill, but the bathroom can still be inconvenient and awkward to use – even the expensive fittings themselves may not really work well.

The real solution lies in careful design that takes every aspect of the use of the room and fittings into account. It is worth remembering that a couple of hundred pounds saved on fittings could buy a solid week's worth of a qualified architects or designer's time – which would surely be money better spent.

The bright red towel, shower curtain, carpet, ceiling and taps make strong splashes of colour in this bathroom with its white walls and fittings. The window has a plain white roller blind.

MICHAEL NEWTON

Disabled users

A great deal of attention has been given in recent years to the problems of disabled people, both in public buildings and in the home. Particular problems occur where facilities have to be shared by disabled people and others, and this is often true when, for example, an elderly person shares a house with a younger family.

As far as the bathroom is concerned, it is obviously sensible to provide for any types of disability that are likely to affect present and potential users, particularly in view of the hazards that exist in terms of slippery surfaces and so on. Elderly people are obviously the most likely users of the average domestic bathroom who can be considered as disabled. The very young provide other problems mentioned elsewhere.

Selwyn Goldsmith, in his book *Designing for the Disabled*, published by the RIBA, goes into considerable detail in discussing the problems associated with the old and the disabled and the way in which solutions to them can conflict with features desired by the young and the able-bodied. Should you need to make special arrangements for disabled users in a bathroom you should study his suggestions and those of the Disabled Living Foundation. Addresses are given in the back of this book. Briefly, however, the average age of the population is getting older and it seems only prudent to take this into account. Heights of equipment and cupboards, easily operated handles and taps, grab handles near baths and showers and handrails elsewhere are all things that should be provided.

Do-it-yourself

Any really enthusiastic do-it-yourselfer will want to carry out a lot of the work, but in the case of a bathroom this does pose a number of problems. The need to conform with regulations, particularly in regard to drainage and drain testing; the size and fragility of some of the more costly fittings to be used; and the multitude of different skills required including drainlaying, plumbing, pipe fixing, carpentry, joinery, plastering, tiling, electrical work, as well as floor laying and painting, all combine to make this the most reluctant room in the house to yield to the attacks of the confident amateur. However, the benefits resulting from really careful workmanship and loving attention to detail are well worth having. In particular, detailed fittings and fixtures and such things as a neat fit to floor coverings are well within many people's competence.

Doors

It is usual nowadays in new buildings for flush doors to be fitted. These should conform with BS 459 and are made in various sizes ranging from 600mm to 900mm wide by 2000mm high and are faced with plywood or hardboard. Good quality, plywood-faced doors can be polished or varnished, bringing out the decorative quality of the veneer. Hardboard must be painted. Sliding doors can frequently be useful where space is limited, but they do lack good sound-proofing qualities and the locks and bolts are awkward and more difficult to use. Doors of any size up to 1200mm × 2400mm can be easily made from blockboard. Great care should be taken in choosing handles, bolts and other 'furniture'. By spending somewhat more than the minimum, the whole quality of the house can be improved, particularly by choosing co-ordinated fittings. Good quality hinges also enhance the door. Lacquered brass, or nylon-washered aluminium alloy hinges should be considered for the bathroom, particularly if the door is to be polished rather than painted, as these are rust resisting and do not require paint protection against the steam.

Drainage

This is the one factor that, more than any other, determines the position of fittings, the ability to alter or add equipment at a later date, and even the siting of the bathroom itself. The basic problem stems from the necessity, for health and safety reasons, to connect a WC to a 100mm diameter watertight drain. Where the bathroom is on an upper floor a 100mm diameter soil or soil and vent pipe is required. These are awkward and intractable fixtures whatever they are made from. They can be cast iron, plastics, copper, lead or fireclay, but cast iron and plastics are by far the most commonly used materials. The vent pipe, which is now often combined with the soil pipe in a modern installation, must be open to the air at high level, above the highest windows of the house.

Drainage is one aspect of your bathroom planning where the advice of your local building inspector will be vital. You are, in fact, required to have his approval before making any alterations to the drains. Different situations will require different solutions, but there are some common factors that should be kept in mind. For example, it is now considered good practice to run soil pipes internally in a duct to avoid freezing in cold weather, and the same applies to other down-pipes. This also eliminates open hoppers in the waste system, which can accumulate leaves and old tennis balls, so there may be something to be said for bringing an old drainage system up-to-date as part of a major bathroom planning exercise. The main soil pipe from the WC will go straight to the drains from the house, with a manhole and cover for access. The joint between the WC and the soil pipe socket should be made with a flexible mastic or a special plastics soil connector to cope with any settlement or movement in the building.

Drying

Drying clothes that have been washed, either in the bathroom or elsewhere, must sometimes take place in the bathroom. Several patent pull-out washing line devices are available and can be incorporated neatly over the bath if thought is taken over the fixing arrangements.

As far as drying the body is concerned, the old-fashioned chromium plated heated towel rail takes a lot of beating as a way of keeping bath mat and towels dry and warm. Drying washing might entail the fitting of a drying machine, either a spin dryer or a tumble dryer (see Laundries). These machines, do, however, produce a lot of vapour and condensation, and mechanical ventilation should be considered, and may well prove essential. Many machines now have a special venting kit available as an accessory, which can be led through an open window or a special hole in an outside wall.

Floors

The choice of floor finishes suitable for bathroom use is extensive; carpets are discussed separately under their own heading on page 37. Alternatives to carpet include linoleum, in either sheet or tile form; vinyl sheet or tiles; glazed or unglazed clay tiles; and cork, which may be in sheets, tiles or specially vinyl coated.

If fitted carpeting is rejected, the most attractive finish in many ways is natural cork, which not only provides a warm-coloured floor but is also warm to the touch. Traditional linoleum is also quite warm to the feet, as it is made from cork; some more modern materials such as vinyl or vinyl asbestos in sheet or tile form tend to feel rather colder.

A wide variety of attractive mosaic and ceramic tile designs are available in different sizes, shapes and patterns. Ceramic tiles have a quality that is lacking in other bathroom flooring materials and in warm climates they come into their own. In this country, however, their attractive appearance is offset by their coldness and in any case they need to be laid on a strong, stable floor. They are excellent though where an under-floor heating system is installed.

Prices vary enormously, but most bathroom floors are not very large, so that a difference of, say, £2 per square metre between cheap tiles and expensive ones will only add about £20 to the bill in material costs. Bearing in mind the amount of use the bathroom floor gets, this can usually be found by economising on some of the fittings. It is generally accepted that cutting costs on floor finishes is a false economy.

Heating

The way in which your house is heated will obviously affect the way you heat the bathroom, but you can vary the heating arrangements to suit the special needs of bathing. Firstly, you will need some general background heat in order to keep the structure and fittings at a reasonable temperature all the time. Secondly, you will probably need some supplementary heat to boost the temperature when the room is in use. Thirdly, you may need a special heat source to cope with condensation and heavy steaming up of mirrors.

Many modern central heating systems have come to rely too much on warm air as the main means of providing comfort. Unfortunately, extremely high air temperatures are needed by some more chilly people to achieve bodily comfort. As a result, many domestic and office buildings provide conditions of overheated discomfort for many of the occupants. A balance of radiant heat and convected warm air is generally a better arrangement and, strangely enough, the old-fashioned hot water radiator system achieves quite a satisfactory balance.

In the bathroom the heated towel rail is in effect a small radiator and when, as was customary, it is connected to the domestic hot water circuit rather than the central heating circuit, it provides warmth to the bathroom and the towels, and, what is most important, the bath mat all through the summer months as well as the winter – at a cost. It is arguable, however, whether alternative methods are any more economical. Economy is best achieved by a judicious use of the thermostat and the time clock.

Other methods exist, of course, but it is certainly advisable to have some sort of background heat, perhaps off the central heating circuit with a booster in the form of an infra-red heater or a warm air blower; this latter, if mounted over the mirror, can remedy any condensation on the glass. There is a combined warm air heater and overhead light unit on the market which is extremely effective when used in this way. Infra-red heaters, although effective, are visually extremely difficult to incorporate into a bathroom.

It is possible to obtain finned hot water pipes that act as miniature radiators when connected to a central heating system and can be concealed behind fascias. There are many types of flat panel radiator and it is worth remembering that these need not necessarily be mounted in exactly the way your local plumber may suggest. Vertical mounting up a wall is one possible arrangement where space is limited, or they can be sited along the side of the bath. Individual tubular electric heaters are cheap to buy; thermostatically controlled, oil-filled radiators and towel rails are more expensive but are worth considering, particularly as they are relatively economical to run. Ideally, the waste heat from the fridge or freezer could be taken advantage of, and no better use could be found for this than as background heat for a bathroom. Any appliance of this sort operates by dissipating waste heat into the atmosphere and a back to back arrangement of freezer and bathroom would be a very satisfying solution.

Hot water cylinders

Hot water storage is now generally provided by a copper cylinder. These vary in capacity from 74 to 450 litres – a bath-full is equivalent to about 90 litres – and must conform to BS 699. There are special cylinders on the market that incorporate their own cold water header tank, which can be useful where no tank already exists or for flats where one may want to avoid having several supplies from tanks in the roof.

The siting of the hot water cylinder is important, whether in the bathroom or outside it, but even more important is the height of the cold water tank above the highest fitting. This provides the 'head' of water needed to provide adequate water pressure, and is critical in the case of a shower, which will need about 1·5m head for satisfactory operation. It is worth siting the hot water cylinder as close as possible to the various draw-off points to save a long wait while water comes through. This will also save fuel.

The hot water storage cylinder should be lagged for fuel economy; under the latest Building Regulations 75mm of insulating quilt is required. Even better, perhaps, are the specially insulated hot water cylinders that are sold complete. It is extremely convenient to have an electrical immersion heater fitted to the storage cylinder, either as a primary or secondary method of water heating. Water heating systems are discussed on page 62.

Ironmongery

This is the rather old-fashioned name given by the trade to all those items of brass, aluminium, stainless steel and even plastics, that are used to open and shut doors, windows and so on. Locks, door handles, window catches, hat and coat hooks are probably the most relevant ones to the planning of your bathroom. This is a trade where tradition and craftsmanship still play an important part; good locks are still largely hand made, while door handles vary from the cheapest aluminium or plastics to bronze or good quality stainless steel.

As far as your bathroom is concerned, you may be able to have completely new fittings throughout and, if this is the case, there are several matching ranges, mostly made in anodised aluminium. Many alternative designs are available if you are only thinking of the odd handle or bolt, but there is no doubt that a co-ordinated set comprising a handle, bolt, hook and so on will add a feeling of quality to the finished room. As with many other aspects of the building industry, it is necessary to take a little extra effort to get what you want, rather than being fobbed off with whatever your local supplier has available. It is a good idea to use aluminium alloy hinges, for example, if your door is to be polished or varnished, and special washered hinges add to the smooth action of the door. You should also choose the types of bolt to be used carefully. There are several designs available that not only indicate whether the room is occupied, by word or colour symbol, but also allow the bolt to be operated from the outside by using a special key or, probably more sensibly, by using an ordinary coin. Any parent who has had to try from the outside to instruct a panic-stricken toddler how to unlock the loo door will appreciate the sense of this device.

Hat and coat hooks with rubber buffers to act as door stops are also useful. Sliding doors, which are frequently aids to compact planning, pose particular problems with door handles and locks, the normal recessed handles being particularly awkward to use. It may well be better to incorporate a special feature such as a purpose-made handle and door stop running the full height of the door and thus eliminate the standard handle. To lock a sliding door you will need either a hook bolt latch or a patent spring-open bolt, both types being key operated.

Sliding door mechanisms vary from the cheap and just workable to those of Rolls Royce quality. Choose the best that you can afford; a badly running sliding door is a permanent irritation. Patent sliding folding plastics doors should be viewed with suspicion; they seldom work as easily as they should. The best way to examine fittings is probably to visit your nearest Building Centre, where samples are on permanent display.

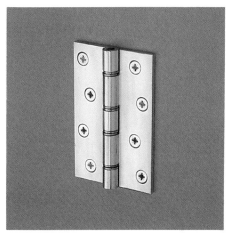

Fittings from the Allgood Modric range available in silver anodised and also in coloured finishes. Top left: indicator with emergency release. Top right: plate and turn for bathroom lock. Bottom left: door hinge and bottom right: buffer hat and coat hook.

Laundry

Some people advocate washing clothes in the bathroom, rather than in the kitchen and, assuming no laundry room or utility room exists it is sensible to consider this arrangement. Firstly, there is a considerable point in doing this if laundry is generally dried over the bath, but somehow the intrusion of a washing machine into the bathroom is incongruous and in any case presents problems of electrical safety : electrical machines must be connected direct to the mains supply rather than an open socket in the bathroom. It may well be feasible to arrange a small laundry recess, perhaps as a lobby to the bathroom, with a louvred door and airing racks over. Obviously the general arrangement of the house will influence a decision such as this, as will the family habits ; muddy football shorts probably ought to be washed as near to the entrance to your house as possible. Laundry and household cleaning are as much a part of living as eating or watching television, but most homes do not accommodate these activities in a satisfactory way. Once again, it is space that is the real luxury, and any plan that can gain useful space is the one to aim at. An alternative arrangement would be to have a laundry area associated with a downstairs secondary bathroom or shower unit, to be used by guests or children, leaving the upstairs bathroom for more relaxed uses. As in all these decisions it is best to sit down calmly in advance and decide what your family really needs, rather than opting for some conventional solution based on habit.

A washing machine and a tumbler drier are fitted neatly below the vanitory basin unit in this bathroom belonging to Mr and Mrs Wilkinson, hidden behind doors and wired to sealed waterproof electric sockets.

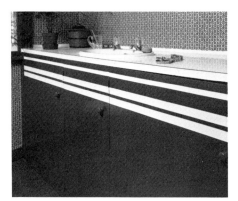

TOM BIRO

Lighting

The purposes of bathroom lighting can be defined very specifically, which helps when it comes to choosing fittings and their position in the bathroom. Lighting is discussed in some detail in the section on bathroom planning, in the first part of this book, and you will also find the Design Centre book on *Planning your lighting* by Derek Phillips of help here, but it is as well to consider the type of fittings that will be needed.

The two main requirements in a bathroom are to provide good face lighting where it is needed, at the mirror for example, and to have a good general standard of illumination throughout the rest of the room. The important thing about face lighting is that the whole of the face should be well lit. To achieve this the light source must be mounted on the wall to which the mirror itself is fixed. Strip-lighting in the form of tungsten or fluorescent tubes is satisfactory, but only if the fitting is long enough to cast light on the sides of the face as well as the front. A short, 300mm fitting, which means most of those made specifically for the purpose with a built-in electric shaver socket, will tend to light the upper surfaces of the face and leave the sides and lower parts under-lit. Lights on each side of the mirror are much better and there are many suitable strip-lights and opal glass or plastics tungsten fittings for this purpose. Some mirrors are made with concealed strip-lights that shine through translucent strips on each side; this is an excellent solution and it can be duplicated using any size mirror with a bit of ingenuity. Some bathroom cabinets also incorporate mirror lighting.

In a very small bathroom, if plenty of light is provided at the mirror over the basin it may well be that, depending on its position, this will light the rest of the room adequately and no further lighting is needed. Usually, however, at least one other source of light is desirable. This is best provided by a ceiling or wall fitting, depending on the size and shape of the room. Generally speaking, the room lighting should 'balance' the mirror lighting so that between them they light the whole room satisfactorily. It is important, however, to make sure that no strong lights reflect in the mirror behind the person using it, as this will reduce the effectiveness of the mirror lighting.

Some people like to read in the bath, and this and other factors should be taken into account when siting the general light sources. A wide variety of translucent fittings are suitable; recessed fittings are more sophisticated but they will generally not spread the light as widely as surface-mounted fittings. They also tend to be rather more expensive to buy and, of course, install. The fact that they are also a rather more costly way of providing a given level of light may not be so critical in a bathroom, where the lights tend to be used for comparatively short periods of time.

Where there is space and you have the opportunity to do so, it is possible to let yourself go and aim at the kind of lighting effects more commonly met within other rooms, with lighting from concealed sources to give atmosphere and, perhaps, spotlights for features such as plants or pictures, should your ideas on bathroom design run to it.

Lighting switches must, of course, be safe to use in the bathroom and this means either having the familiar pull cord from a switch mounted on the ceiling or, alternatively, mounting switches outside the room altogether.

Make-up

A male writer is at risk if he ventures to lay down any criteria for designing for making up. However, for many years the theatrical profession has had to make up in difficult and uncomfortable dressing rooms, and the standard theatre arrangement of bare tungsten lamps surrounding a mirror has a lot to commend it. The problem remains – how to provide good artificial lighting that also looks visually attractive? Most specially designed fittings are in fact unsatisfactory. The intensity of the light is inadequate and the direction is wrong. If a vanitory unit is to be included, special lighting is not too difficult to incorporate, but the whole design needs careful thought to be successful and some experimentation may be necessary. Diffusing glass panels with lights behind them on either side of a large mirror and possibly above can be reasonably effective. The use of a dimmer switch together with a number of lamps could also be satisfactory as the most intense light then need only be used when actually required, but this would have to be positioned outside the room for safety.

Materials for sanitary fittings

The materials from which the main sanitary fittings are now made are:

for baths
Porcelain enamelled cast iron
Vitreous enamelled pressed steel
Acrylic plastics
Glass fibre reinforced polyester resin (GRP)

for basins, bidets and WCs
Glazed earthenware
Vitreous china
Glazed fireclay
Acrylic plastics
Stainless steel

for shower trays
Vitreous china
Vitreous enamelled pressed steel
Glazed fireclay
Acrylic plastics and GRP

The manufacture of a porcelain enamelled bath entails the fusing, at very high temperature, of powdered glass and other chemicals in successive layers onto the cast iron body of the bath. The result is a robust, thick coating of opaque glaze which is more or less permanent.

Porcelain enamelled cast iron is an excellent material for baths, being durable and of good appearance. Colours are available from most manufacturers.

Vitreous enamelled pressed steel baths are manufactured by the application of ground glass, pigments and other chemicals mixed with water and sprayed as a slurry onto the pressed steel body of the bath. The water is dried out and the whole heated to about 830°C to melt the coating. The result is a material that is resistant to scratching, acids and impact damage and retains its high gloss for a very long time.

Acrylic plastics can be used in sheet form to manufacture large items of sanitary ware by heating to 150–170°C when the material becomes stretchable and pliable. The material can then be formed into a variety of shapes and many colours are available. The more exotically shaped baths are often made from this material, the one major disadvantage being its susceptibility to cigarette burns.

GRP is used particularly for the more experimental shapes as small quantities of any particular design can be made reasonably economically. Its characteristics are similar to those of acrylic baths. Manufacturers are now combining the two processes to strengthen the acrylic bath by reinforcement with glass fibres.

Glazed earthenware was once commonly used for the smaller fittings, but its use is now virtually discontinued. Although cheap, there was a tendency to craze as the porous clay under the glaze would swell with any water penetration.

Vitreous china is most often used for the smaller items. The process is complex and begins with a white body of a mixture of ball clay, china clay, flint or sand, and felspar. This is poured into a mould and then removed while still soft, dried naturally for several days, and finally spray glazed, fired and cooled. The material is excellent for basins, WCs, bidets and other items up to the size of a shower tray. Above this size the material is likely to distort.

Glazed fireclay is manufactured from a mixture of deep mined refractory clays which gives a thicker body of higher strength than vitreous china. The body colour is a dark buff and a vitreous china slip has to be applied before glazing. Items of a much larger size can be manufactured but the drying out process is longer and the resultant fittings more expensive. The material is heavy and is being superseded by other materials. However several unique designs are still made from glazed fireclay, including a one-piece shelf basin.

Coloured finishes are available in all these materials, but it is worth inspecting fittings made from different materials closely in the showroom as a perfect match can be difficult to achieve.

Mirrors

Conventional polished plate glass mirrors are quite satisfactory for use in bathrooms, although it is worth taking certain precautions to ensure that damp cannot penetrate to the silvering on the back. A soft rubber or plastics foam strip stuck all round the edge of the back of the mirror should solve this problem and also cushion it against the wall. Care should be taken in fixing large mirrors in particular, so that unequal stresses are not induced, leading to cracking.

As an alternative to glass mirrors, flexible reflective plastics sheeting can be obtained. This can be mounted on chipboard and used to provide reflective wall surfaces in a variety of colours.

Small shaving mirrors with integral lights are readily available, but as with all such devices, the practical usefulness of the accessory seems to be inversely proportional to its looks – in other words, the more convenient, the more unsightly. Designers need to solve this problem more effectively than they have yet done.

The currently fashionable coloured mirrors in this bathroom are matched with warm paint colours, contrasting with simple white fittings.

TIM STREET-PORTER/LIZ WHITING

Pipes

There is nothing more important in achieving a visually satisfactory bathroom than concealing the pipework. In nearly all the examples illustrated in this book this has been done and the results speak for themselves. Some architects, due to their early functionalist upbringing, like to expose, or as it is sometimes called 'express', the pipework; this can be effective in really large industrial buildings, where the brightly colour coded pipework is a feature of the plant room. In your domestic bathroom such exposure is more likely to offend; there will be a mass of bends, connectors, fittings and so on, which will give an impression of untidiness. There is something appealing about highly polished copper and brass as seen in the better quality public lavatory or hotel toilet. This is due perhaps to the feeling of old-fashioned loving care, or naval associations, rather than any intrinsic aesthetic qualities.

Copper, galvanised steel, and stainless steel are all used for hot and cold water supply pipes, while pvc or polythene can be used for cold water and waste pipes. There seems little advantage in departing from the conventional materials, particularly where the quantities of pipework involved are comparatively small. Price differentials between alternative materials vary from year to year. Pipework in lead has now largely ceased to be used in domestic installations.

Concealing the pipework presents certain difficulties and these can best be overcome by some sort of ducting. In building terminology a duct is a vertical or horizontal space that conceals pipes, wires, conduits, etc. In the bathroom itself, horizontal ducting to hide the hot and cold water pipes can be built using timber framing, and covered with a choice of materials, such as painted or plastics-faced plywood or boarding. Access must be provided for maintenance and repairs, so that neatly designed fixings will be needed. The vertical soil pipe must be hidden if it has to be located in the bathroom and again access should be possible. Concealed fixing devices are available and concealed hinges make for a tidy solution. Rows of cups and screws, although commonly used, are unsightly and irritating to deal with in an emergency. A professional designer will achieve a good-looking result by detailing the joints in the access panels in such a way that they are co-ordinated with the design of the room as a whole.

Exposed pipework must be carefully laid out and installed to be effective, and even then may not be to everyone's taste.
Architects Stout & Litchfield

Planning and planners

These poor words have now acquired an almost pejorative meaning, stemming from the frustrations often met with by the citizen in trying to deal with the planning authorities. In fact, in planning your bathroom you will not need to be involved with the planners unless you are altering the external appearance of your house, by, for example, inserting a new window, or if you live in a listed building (on the List of Buildings of Architectural or Historical Interest). In this case you will need listed building consent to alter the building even if you are not altering the external appearance. If you live in a conservation area you should take advice if you wish to alter your house, as it may be on a list currently being prepared. In any case, there should be no difficulty in obtaining planning permission, although this can take at least two months. Planning permission must not be confused with Building Regulation approval, which will be required if you are altering drainage and so on. Should you be adding an extension to your house, then planning permission from your local council will probably be needed. Application forms and drawings will have to be provided and you will almost certainly require professional help in preparing these.

You should note that improvements to your house, other than installing central heating, should not affect its rateable value, but an addition or extension to the house almost certainly will.

Safety

More accidents occur in the home than in any other place of work, and many of the most serious take place in the bathroom. For obvious reasons the hazards in a bathroom are more extreme, with the combination of water, electricity, and possibly gas, and the lack of protective clothing. Sensible people will avoid open-fronted electric power sockets, unventilated gas water heaters and other dangerous fixtures, but there are quite easy measures that can be taken to eliminate the less obvious hazards. Children and old people are particularly at risk and it seems only sensible that grab handles and non-slip surfaces should be incorporated into every bathroom, and not only into those designed for the old or disabled. Most good electricians will refuse to install unsafe electrical systems into bathrooms, but there is no such guarantee with other trades. The Royal Society for the Prevention of Accidents has this to say:

'It is particularly important to guard against the use of portable electrical appliances in the bathroom, in particular such things as record players, electric hair dryers, and electric fires, plugged into an open fronted power point. Do-it-yourselfers are particularly prone to dangerous electrical installations. Other important points include the necessity to ensure good ventilation whenever there is a gas water heater, and the vital need to make certain that the old, infirm or very young are always supervised in the bathroom.'

Saunas and suchlike

Saunas, solaria, and impulse showers are, we think, beyond the scope of this book. Anyone considering such luxuries will be prepared to spend at least £1000 and will be thinking about far more than the bathroom. It may well be sensible to consider these installations in conjunction with a bathroom, however, and several specialist firms will be able to advise on them.

Showers and shower cubicles

Showers have become an increasingly popular alternative, or at any rate addition, to baths in recent years and they offer several advantages, being quicker, more economical on water and fuel, and more hygienic into the bargain.

The initial decision when considering installing a separate shower or adding one to an existing bathroom is whether the hot water supply system provides enough pressure or 'head'. Pressure is determined by the position of the cold water tank (not the hot water cylinder as you might expect) and there should be at the very least 1·2m between the draw-off point on the cold water tank and the highest outlet in the bathroom, which is generally the shower. Less than this and the results will be very disappointing and some mixers will not operate below about 1·5m head. Electric pumps are available to boost pressure as a last resort.

The next decision is whether to have the shower installed above the bath or to have a separate shower cubicle, which may be a proprietary unit or can be specially built on a ready-made base. It is, of course, easier to integrate a specially built shower into the rest of the bathroom, and fittings can be chosen to match those elsewhere in the room. The basic requirement is a shower tray, which can be made from vitreous china, vitreous enamelled pressed steel, glazed fireclay, acrylic plastics or GRP. These are fairly easily installed in combination with waterproofing of nearby walls by means of ceramic tiles or other finishes. A curtain or door will be needed to avoid splashing the rest of the room.

Shower cubicles can be bought complete with all fittings, including a seat in some cases, which is a useful thing to have in any shower. They are, however, often not very attractive to look at and may be difficult to integrate into the room as a whole. They can be most useful for installing in a guest bedroom or a downstairs cloakroom where additional facilities are required. It is possible to provide a miniature second bathroom, complete with WC, shower and basin, in an area 1065mm by 2000mm in this way.

Shower controls can be either manual or automatic, whether or not they are combined with the taps for the bath. There is a lot to be said for automatic, thermostatic controls, which provide water at a constant temperature irrespective of the hot water temperature and pressure. Once set, there is no need to juggle with hot and cold taps to get the temperature you need, and they are an important safety precaution where children or old persons use a shower. Controls for separate, step-in showers can be recessed into the wall and hidden, which looks particularly neat.

Small, instant electrically heated shower heaters are available for use with mains pressure water supply, but their installation must be approved by the local water authority.

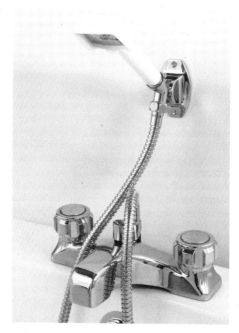

Left: Armitage Shanks Starlite, a combined bath and shower mixer incorporating an automatic valve that reverts to the 'bath' position when the shower is turned off. Centre and right: two versions of Leonard thermostatic showers made by Walker Crosweller & Co combining temperature and flow control. The flexible hose version offers a choice of positions.

Below left: Ideal Standard shower tray with Idealmix fitting with two height positions for outlet.
Below right: Carron Calypso 4 with acrylic side panels, curtain rail and single white curtain. The height of the shower outlet is adjusted by sliding the fitting up or down, and the water is heated by a thermostatic controller.

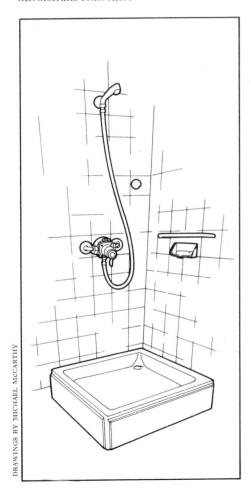

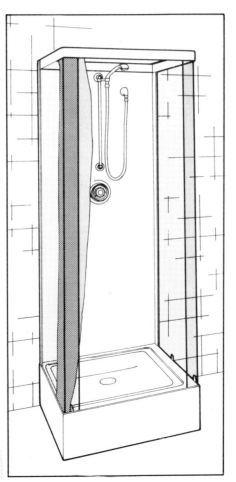

DRAWINGS BY MICHAEL MCCARTHY

Sizes and shapes

There are three aspects of this subject that are worth considering: the size and shape of the bathroom as a whole; that of the items of equipment in it; and finally of the people who use it. In each case we are touching on the field of ergonomics – the ugly name given to the study of man in relation to machines, tools and other artifacts.

To start with the room itself, a considerable amount of work has been done on investigating people's reactions to the bathrooms they use. The results of some of this work are published in a useful booklet from the Department of the Environment entitled *Design Bulletin No 24. Spaces in the home – Bathrooms and WCs*. The main conclusion, based on an investigation of over 900 households, approximately half of which were owner-occupied, was that inadequate size was the chief source of dissatisfaction with bathrooms, aggravated by bad planning of the room itself. These findings generally related to one-bathroom households, which suggests that you should be particularly careful if you propose to have a single small bathroom of, say, 3·75 square metres or less for your whole family. Another point that emerges clearly from the survey is that care must be taken in siting the various fittings in a bathroom so that there is adequate space around them for convenience. Most of the bathrooms studied were, in fact, on the small side – 2·1 × 2·0m or so.

The question of size of room is, of course, greatly affected by use and, should there be only two people in a family, the problem will not be particularly acute. If there are some children of school age, however, congestion will almost certainly arise. The solution is unlikely to lie within the walls of a single bathroom; a WC in the bathroom plus another one elsewhere and a washbasin in a separate cloakroom or bedroom will be far more use than simply a larger bathroom.

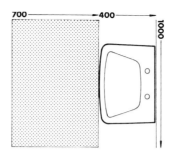

Basins are generally 600 × 400mm and about 800mm high, although this can be raised to 900mm for adults. They need a clear space 1000 × 700mm in front of them for comfortable use.

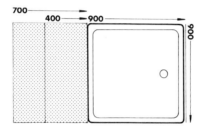

Showers are usually either 800 × 800mm or 900 × 900mm square and the shower tray needs to be at least 150mm high. Showers enclosed on one or two sides should have a clear space of 400 × 900mm in front of them for access and drying. Those enclosed on three sides need a larger area 700 × 900mm.

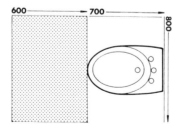

Bidets usually measure 700 × 400mm. They need a clear floor space 800 × 600mm in front of them and this should extend back to the wall for most models to give leg and elbow space. Height is generally 400mm.

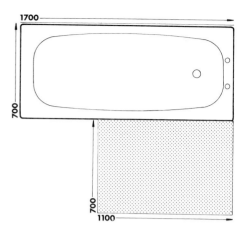

Baths are generally 1700 × 700mm with a rim height of between 500mm and 600mm. The adjacent clear floor space should be 1100 × 700mm with the longer dimension next to the bath, preferably at the tap end.

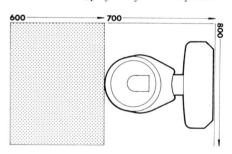

WCs generally fit within a space 700 × 400mm, although most cisterns are longer than this. There should be a clear activity space 800 × 600mm measured from the front lip of the pan. Height of pan is generally 400mm.

In terms of equipment, it is interesting to note that many of the standard dimensions of such things as baths, basins, WCs, vanitory units and so on are not altogether satisfactory. The problem here arises from the concept of an average-sized man, woman or child, on which manufacturers necessarily have to base their designs in many cases. It needs only a moment's thought to realise that the idea of a standard size of shoe, representing the average of all the large and small foot sizes, would only be of use to a small percentage of the population. The same applies, to some extent, to the average height for basins and baths. You should therefore think carefully whether some variation from the norm might suit your particular family requirements, and consider choosing fittings of non-standard height if you can find them – some designs are more flexible than others in terms of the way in which they can be fitted. Accessories, mirrors, cupboards and so on should all be sited in convenient places for those who will actually use the bathroom, with alternative positions for some items if necessary.

As an aid to planning, the average dimensions of the main items of bathroom equipment are shown on the left, together with the amount of space that each needs next to it for convenient use. These 'activity spaces' can be a bit flexible and can overlap to some extent – where a basin is at a different height from a WC, for instance, or where two adjacent fittings are unlikely to be used at the same time by different people.

Taps

In recent years taps have been the subject of much re-design by manufacturers. Unfortunately, to the mind of those influenced by the ideals of the Bauhaus and the Modern Movement, most of this re-designing has been more in the nature

of cosmetic treatment than true design. Obviously there have been improvements, but many of the real problems associated with using taps seem to have been ignored. It is still awkward and difficult to clean many of the super looking taps shown in the advertisements, and they are still difficult to re-washer. Onyx heads and a gold plated finish do not improve the working of the tap. Some designs can also be difficult and even painful to turn, especially with hands slippery from soap or shampoo.

Nevertheless, there is quite a lot of choice. For your bath you can have individual taps mounted either on the bath or the wall; mixer units mounted on the bath or the wall; mixer units with shower attachments; or thermostatic mixers activating either shower, bath or handspray for hair washing. It is possible to obtain combined bath and shower

There are several different types of tap to choose from. The three on the left are all from Armitage Shanks and are a simple Nisaline chrome plated, brass, pillar tap, and two versions of the Clarendon Nu-flo mixer tap, both with pop-up waste controls and insulated grip rings. The picture above is of a combined hot and cold mixer spray tap by Walker Crosweller & Co.

mixers that automatically return to bath supply after the shower is switched off, thus avoiding the unexpected drenching of an unsuspecting guest or mother about to bath the baby.

For your basin, individual taps or mixer taps can be chosen, again either basin-mounted or wall-mounted. Surgeons' lever-operated taps give a very positive action and are a pleasure to use, although some water authorities do not favour them. Single-lever spray taps of a variety of designs are also available for basins, the temperature and flow of the water being controlled by the positioning of the tap head. Most manufacturers make co-ordinated ranges of taps to match all the fittings in the bathroom. Generally speaking it is wise to select such a range for your bathroom if you are starting from scratch.

The combined bath mixer and shower below is a chrome plated version of the range of Vola bathroom fittings designed by the Danish architect, Arne Jacobsen, also made in a range of coloured finishes.

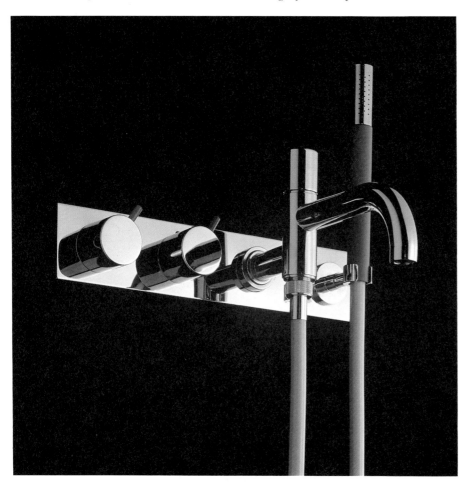

Towel rails

The well fitted bathroom fifty years ago would have had a heated towel rail run off the hot water system and made from chromium plated brass with the familiar swollen-shaped junction pieces – all of a generous diameter, ideal for ensuring that the huge Turkish towels were warm and dry. There has not been much, if any, improvement on this arrangement. However, smaller bathrooms have necessitated smaller towel rails and these are made in chromium plated tubing in a wide range of sizes, both floor-standing and wall-mounted, for connecting to a hot water central heating system. This remains a good way of heating the bathroom generally and keeping the towels dry and warm at the same time. The heated towel rail can either be connected to the central heating proper, in which case it will not operate during the summer, or to the hot water system. In the latter case it will operate all the year round but can of course be turned off if not wanted.

Towel rails are available for clipping on to radiators. These do a good job where a radiator rather than a heated towel rail is installed. They do not provide as much hanging space as a heated towel rail, which can have several rails. On the other hand, for bathrooms above a certain size, a radiator will heat the room more satisfactorily. Your heating engineer can advise you. If your heating system is a warm air one then you can fit a towel rail above the outlet grille. Electric towel rails do the same job as hot water rails and are available both as heated towel rails for wall mounting and as oil-filled, floor-standing radiators with a multiple towel rail above. The wall-mounted models are generally of very low loading – 100 to 120 watts – and therefore use little more electricity than the average light bulb. Some of these are oil-filled as are the radiators. The radiator models have built-in thermostats and so can be set to run economically. Nonetheless, with the cost

Above and right: Both these bathrooms make imaginative use of towel rails. In the first one, the serpentine towel rail has been made up specially from ordinary copper tube and chromium plated. Spotlights are set into the wall for make-up purposes. On the right, Nicholas Hills' bathroom has two traditional hot-water towel rails, one at each end of the bath, set at right angles to the wall. The tiles are his own design.

of electricity over other fuels, it would be as well to have electric towel rails wired to a time clock to avoid using them unnecessarily at night or when the house is empty, and yet have the bathroom warm when it is needed.

Unheated towel rails are available in chrome brass and bronze, anodised aluminium, coloured epoxy resin on brass, plastics, and other materials. They are made as parts of ranges of ironmongery and bathroom fittings so that, depending on which kind of design and finish you favour, they can match your other accessories and taps. Towel rings, as opposed to rails, are useful for small hand towels adjacent to basins and can be fitted in spaces that are too small to take a rail. They frequently feature in advertisers' photographs but they do have disadvantages: the process of extracting and inserting the towel is more tedious than with a towel rail as the towel has to be folded narrowly and this also prevents it from drying properly.

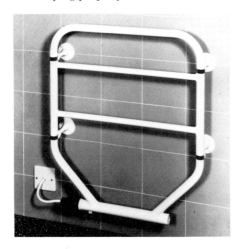

Left: Electric towel rails are easily incorporated into most bathrooms. This wall-mounted version in white stove enamel is by Dimplex Ltd. An alternative is to use materials that match those elsewhere in the bathroom, as with simple timber one shown above. Architect Peter Aldington

Valves

Valves or stopcocks fitted in a length of pipe can be used to isolate fittings from the water supply and regulate the flow of water. With the ever increasing cost of labour it makes sense to fit stop valves to every tap as standard whether hot or cold. This allows the re-washering of the taps either by the householder, or, if necessary, by a visiting plumber who will need very little time to carry out the work, as he will not need to drain down the system. Such stop valves can be chromium plated if exposed, or hidden behind an access panel. Isolating valves in the pipes to and from the cold water tank and in the domestic hot water circuit should also be fitted. A regulating valve fitted in the water supply to a WC may help to quieten it if it is noisy.

Vanitory units

This is the now generally accepted, but nevertheless rather unpleasant, name given to wash basins built into a counter-top. There are certain obvious advantages in this arrangement and some not so obvious snags. The design does without doubt tidy up some of the problems associated with a wash-basin used as a place for make up and all the other bits and pieces associated with cleaning teeth, shaving, washing and so on. The design hides the plumbing and waste pipes and gives a thought-out look to the room. Vanitory units are particularly popular when incorporated into a dressing room as opposed to a conventional bathroom.

The snags arise from the detailed fitting of a basin into a smooth flat surface. Readers must judge for themselves how well the various manufacturers have handled this problem. Perhaps a cleaner, more elegant solution lies in the choice of a one-piece shelf basin. Some manufacturers supply oval-shaped basins that fit under a plastics laminate-faced shelf, while others make basins that fit into shelves with a front overhang. It is feasible to select an alternative to plastics laminate for the shelf surface itself. Polished marble, slate, highly compressed asbestos cement, or polished terrazzo are all satisfactory, though expensive, materials. Your local monumental mason can probably oblige with a choice of marbles. In the case of natural slate or marble the thickness of the stone can be above 30mm giving a robust edge thickness around the basin cut-out and on the face, but the slab will, of course, be very heavy.

Ventilation

Good ventilation is one of the most important aims in a bathroom, not only to eliminate such obviously unpleasant things as smells and steam, but also to help avoid heavy condensation and the harmful effects that persistent condensation can have on such things as curtains, wallpaper, electrical fittings and clothes. Permanent ventilation to the open air is not really altogether necessary, but some effective natural ventilation is highly desirable. Extractor fans are inevitably noisy, and frequently produce a noise that is particularly irritating. On the whole, a traditional, well heated bathroom with an opening window and an adjustable wall extract grille, can be almost completely satisfactory, while an internal bathroom with extractor fan, although it may be a more modern idea, is frequently unsatisfactory to use.

When an extractor fan is contained in a ventilation duct the noise can be reduced by careful attention to mounting and acoustic treatment. Switching on and off can be controlled by pull switch or by a door-operated switch.

*This view of the circular bathroom
discussed on page 24 shows the extensive use
of mosaic tiles on walls and other surfaces,
and the vanitory basin fixed beneath a
worktop. The neatly inset ceramic soap-
holders match the wall tiles.
Designer Graham Hopewell*

Walls

Materials for covering and surfacing the walls in your bathroom offer considerable choice. In fact though, assuming that you are dealing with an existing house, your choice will be limited to those materials suitable for applying to plastered brickwork. Traditionally, glazed tiling or mosaic is often favoured. Many exotic colours, patterns and textures are available, both home produced and imported. The attraction of glazed tiling lies in its regularity, and good professional workmanship is essential and often difficult to obtain. Glass mosaic presents a challenge which some will enjoy taking up. By judicious choice of the cheaper background colours such as white and pale grey, with small quantities of exotic gold, yellows, vermilions and blues, your own design can be worked out and placed in position. Mosaic is enhanced by slight irregularities in the surface and extremely rich and exotic effects can be achieved. Grouting the joints is surprisingly easy. Small ceramic mosaics are a different matter and need treating as tiles. Look at the alternative sizes for glazed wall tiles, in particular those that are narrow and tall. The often criticised clinical look can be avoided by avoiding the conventional 150 × 150mm glazed tile and choosing some other size.

Plastered walls can be painted, papered or have timber boarding applied on battens, which will allow pipework to be hidden. Cork can be stuck on in tile or sheet form and is warm to the touch. Wallpaper for bathroom use should, of course, be either waterproof or washable.

Waste fittings

There is some choice in waste fittings for basins and baths, and there are various ways of allowing the waste water to run away. Firstly, if you choose a conventional plug type waste there is only one design that is really satisfactory: this is a trumpet-shaped waste with the name of 'goblet'. This design allows the water to flow away without impediment and does not trap water or any floating bits and pieces around the plug hole. More complicated devices such as the pop-up fixed waste, the foot-operated waste, and so on, also exist; the goblet type waste can be obtained in these forms and will be found to be satisfactory.

The waste fittings connect to drains via traps, which provide a water seal when the fittings are not in use, and here again there is considerable choice. If the basin trap is exposed, as on a cantilever type basin, a chromium plated bottle trap will probably be the best choice, but any good quality trap that can be easily unscrewed for cleaning will be acceptable. The advent of plastics drainage systems means that there are many designs to choose from in this material. Any fitting that is used for washing hair should certainly have its trap cleaned out from time to time. In the case of baths there is frequently very little space for the trap to fit between them and the floor. In this case it is worth fitting a special, shallow trap designed to eliminate syphonage when the bath is emptied and reduce the gurgling noise that syphonage causes.

Water authorities

With local government re-organisation in 1974 the Water Authorities have been re-organised and as statutory undertakings their dictates must be obeyed. The practical effects of their regulations concern the capacity of cold water storage tanks in new buildings; the type of pipework permitted in the rising main into the tank; the type of ball valve fitted in the tank; certain detailed requirements covering mixer taps in kitchens and water waste devices; and whether certain appliances can be connected direct to the mains.

It will probably not be necessary to have direct dealing with the water supply authority unless extensive new work is undertaken; most plumbers are well versed in the quirks of the local water people.

Water heating

'The benison of hot water' is surely the greatest single achievement of civilisation! Arguments rage on the most convenient and economical way of heating the water for one's bathroom – each fuel has its protagonist and the figures can be presented to support whichever case is being made. In practical terms, however, there is not a great deal to choose between oil, gas, solid fuel and electricity, provided that each is used sensibly and that there is adequate lagging of all the pipework and the hot water cylinder. Money spent on insulation is money well spent, and it is also worth planning the bathroom so that there are short runs of hot water pipe from the cylinder to the taps. The temperature at which you set your thermostat is also important; excessively hot water has to have cold water added to it even for washing-up purposes, and it is generally agreed that you should set the temperature only at the hottest bearable level for your individual needs. It is a waste of fuel to be able to make tea straight from the tap or fill your hot water bottle from it, and then have to add cold water to all your washing water.

Several systems for producing hot water are available, many of which involve a copper storage cylinder. These are discussed in more detail on page 44. A cylinder can be heated indirectly as part of a central heating system, with a boiler situated elsewhere in the house. Where it is not possible to incorporate the hot water cylinder into a central heating system, the most usual method of water heating is by an electric immersion heater. A cylinder can be fitted with two immersion heaters,

one at the top to heat a small amount of water relatively quickly and one at the bottom, which will heat all the water in the cylinder but will take a while to do it (hot water tends to rise to the top of the cylinder and cold water falls to the bottom). As a guide, a 3kW immersion heater installed in the bottom of a 160 litre cylinder will take two hours to heat 90 litres of water (enough for the average bath) from 15°C to 70°C.

As mentioned previously, the hot water cylinder must be lagged for fuel economy. This is true for all fuels and methods of heating, but a high standard of lagging is particularly vital in the case of tanks with an immersion heater, as electricity is most expensive. The latest recommendations call for 75mm of insulation around the tank and this is generally done by means of a quilt or jacket. Another, older method is to build a box around the cylinder and fill this with loose vermiculite. This had advantages when jackets were made to lower standards than they are now, but with much thicker modern jackets available, the gap has narrowed. Even better than a lagged cylinder are the specially insulated cylinders on the market that come complete with a high standard of lagging enclosed in their own well finished casing.

Where water is to be heated by electricity only, off-peak 'night storage' heating should be considered. This method involves a special sealed time clock that switches the water heater in the tank on at the start and off at the end of the cheaper, off-peak electricity supply period during the night. A large tank is used so that there is enough water to meet the household's requirements through the day and the cylinder itself is specially designed to minimise turbulence and avoid cold and hot water becoming mixed up inside it. Off-peak systems should have an additional immersion heater wired to the normal electricity supply so that hot water can be obtained reasonably quickly in the case of extra-heavy use or when one returns home after a holiday during which the off-peak system has been turned off.

Storage water heaters fired by gas are also available. These can be controlled by a time clock and thermostat but, unlike electrical systems, gas heaters require a flue to exhaust waste gases and must therefore be sited appropriately so that the flue can pass through an outside wall or through the roof.

Instant water heaters fuelled by gas or electricity can be used and they have the advantages of being relatively cheap to install and only producing hot water when it is required. On the other hand, they are not the cheapest method of producing hot water for a family-sized household. Instant gas water heaters (traditionally known as geysers) are generally sited in full view above the basin, bath or, in the case of the larger, multi-point models, elsewhere in the bathroom. In this case it is important to reduce the length of pipe runs to a minimum and lag them well. Multi-point models can supply all the fittings in a bathroom and even some fittings in other rooms as well, switching on automatically when a tap is turned on. Many gas heaters now have a balanced flue ventilation system, which means that a single hole in an external wall is enough to supply them with air and exhaust their waste gases. Gas water heaters are generally an inelegant way of providing hot water, however. They are usually relatively slow and noisy, and the temperature of the water is largely controlled by the speed at which it is drawn off, whereas in other methods of water heating the temperature is independent. Also, they do not heat water to the temperatures that other methods provide and so cooling of water in pipe runs between the heater and the taps becomes a problem. This is particularly irritating when washing, shaving or washing hair, for example, when one needs to run water several times at intervals.

Electric instant water heaters are available for fitting above a basin, 'geyser fashion' or for installation at low level in, say, a vanitory unit. They do not come in sizes suitable for heating water for baths and their use is likely to be limited to supplying hot water for somewhere like a separate WC where a cold water supply exists or can easily be installed. In this case they do provide a very cheap form of hot water installation.

Showers are dealt with under their own heading on page 52, but it is worth mentioning here that it is far simpler to install a shower where there is a constant hot water supply and an adequate head of water. Small electric shower heaters do, however, exist and can be connected to the mains water supply, subject to water board approval. In this case they are quite a cheap solution.

Water softeners

Many areas suffer from unpleasantly hard water and the use of a water softener should be considered. The better known firms advertise quite widely and will be able to give information on which water authorities supply hard water; such a firm can also provide a suitable water softening installation. The question arises whether this is money well spent. There is no doubt that hard water induces unpleasant scum in baths and basins, and eventually furs up the inside of pipes. It is difficult, however, to prove that the money spent on water softening can be recouped in any measurable way, by, for example, reducing the amount of soap or detergent used in the household wash. We would certainly advocate expenditure of this kind rather than paying for extravagant fittings, which do nothing to increase the performance of the bathroom. Installations vary from small portable kits to large semi-automatic devices requiring quite a large amount of space to house them.

WCs

Water closets come in a number of different sizes and shapes. The pan itself can be made from fireclay, vitreous china or glazed earthenware. Stainless steel is used for vandal-proof public lavatories. Vitreous china is the most popular material and is easily cleaned and hygienic.

WC pans are either wash-down or siphonic; the advantages of the siphonic pan are that the contents are sucked into the drain and the evacuation is complete and effective, and the operation is much quieter. The choice of flushing tank provides some opportunities for departing from convention. The low-level suite is popular but more elegant solutions are available, such as total concealment of the tank or the use of a flushing valve. In the latter case it is necessary to check with the local water board that its use is permitted. There has been a move in the last few years towards a different design of pan of lower, backward-sloping form, which encourages a squatting position. This is supposed to be more natural and to encourage correct bowel movements. The problem arises, if one of these fittings is chosen, not only of finding a supplier but also of providing a more conventional water closet for the old and infirm. Ideally, there should be two WCs per household, a ground floor orthodox one with aids for the disabled, and a low fitting upstairs for those members of the family who are health conscious.

Most people feel that they have done enough by choosing a matching coloured water closet suite and buying a cover for the seat and a matching rug for the floor. In fact there is considerable choice of shape, colour, type and colour of seat, high or low level tank, and so on. The only warning to heed is: be sure if you choose a fashionable colour that you will still like it in five years' time. Look at the fashionable colours of twenty years ago and ask yourself if you still like them. Consider carefully whether a white pan

with colour incorporated into the decorations might not be the best choice. If you decide otherwise, you can go ahead and purchase a water closet with period decorations under the glaze or any colour you like. You might even decorate your own by obtaining the pan before it has been glazed.

The way in which the WC is connected to the soil pipe can vary. All WCs have some form of trap or 'U-bend' to seal them off from the drains, and this can either be roughly horizontal, in which case it is termed a P trap, or vertical, S trap type. The P trap shape can also be obtained angled to left or right, which may suit certain difficult installations and save some space in planning. In any case, you should make sure that you get the right shaped WC for your particular situation; a manufacturer's catalogue will give you the necessary details.

Top: Wash-down WC pan.
Bottom: Syphonic WC pan.

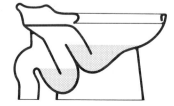

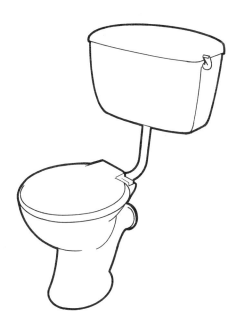

Armitage Shanks Magnia. Typical modern washdown type WC with low level cistern.

Fordham Flush Panel cistern replaces an existing high-level cistern without altering the WC pan position. It is very shallow and takes up little space.

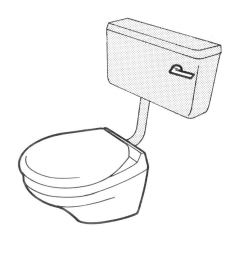

Armitage Shanks Braemar. Wall-hung pan of washdown type with cistern concealed in duct leaving floor free.

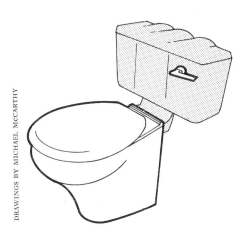

Armitage Shanks Profile. Syphonic WC fitting tight against wall with cistern concealed in duct.

Ideal-Standard Brasilia. Close-coupled syphonic WC with cistern attached avoiding a visible pipe. Cover and seat form an integral part of the design.

DRAWINGS BY MICHAEL McCARTHY

65

Windows

Window design typifies many of the dilemmas inherent in architectural design. Views out are desirable, but entail views in when the light is on; obscured glass obliterates the enjoyable view out on a sunny morning. An opening window certainly allows the rapid extract of steam or unpleasant smells, sometimes useful if the water closet is in the bathroom proper. Internal bathrooms are permissible under regulations assuming adequate artificial ventilation, but psychologically the small internal bathroom is claustrophobic, as anyone will know who has inhabited a modern hotel room. So-called luxury bathrooms illustrated by imaginative advertisers usually assume a completely artificial interior environment cut off from the outside world and resembling a space ship interior. Before accepting such a vision, consideration should be given to the opposite ideal, that of washing and bathing in the open air with the sun warming the naked skin. The window is the device that allows a happy compromise to be achieved. Aspect should, if possible, be east or south, and the window should provide views of the sky; one pane of glass at high level is worth two lower down. If your bathroom is in a roof space there are excellent patent roof windows available that provide most of what is required, including the alternative choice of outside awning, Venetian blind or roller blind, several methods of remote control, and complete ease of cleaning as well as being double glazed and draught sealed.

Opening windows are available in aluminium, steel, wood and plastics; in many instances adjustable glass louvre windows can be fitted which are excellent for adjustment and ventilation. It is best to install these where there is some protection from driving wind or rain, such as overhanging eaves.

*This extension to a cottage in Sussex uses
timber boarding to clad the ceiling and also
to conceal the plumbing. Storage is provided
by simple wooden shelving and a matching
towel rail is mounted above a tubular
electric heater.
Architects Stout & Litchfield*

Guide to manufacturers and products

As with any specialised area, it is often difficult for the ordinary person to find out exactly what is available when planning a bathroom. Builders' merchants and hardware shops often do not have the space to display complete manufacturers' ranges, and not all firms advertise in the press, so choosing fittings and accessories can be a problem. In any case, rather than taking the first thing that's available, you may well want to compare it with other, similar products before deciding.

On the two pages that follow, we have provided a list of the names and addresses of 63 different manufacturers of bathroom equipment, cross-referenced with the types of products they make. Manufacturers with products in the Design Council's Design Index are marked * and can be specially recommended. So if you're looking for a particular type of product, you can simply read off the names of likely manufacturers and get their catalogues and the name of your nearest stockist.

Obviously, the danger of a list like this is that it will become out of date. We have done our best to ensure that it is absolutely accurate at the time of going to press in June 1976, and we hope that its usefulness will outweigh any future shortcomings.

Company	Tel	Accessories	Basins	Baths	Bidets	Cabinets	Shaver Sockets	Shower Cubicles	Shower Fittings	Shower Trays	Taps, Valves & Wastes	Tiles & Fittings	Vanitory Units	WC Cisterns	WC Pans	WC Suites
*G & S Allgood Ltd, 297 Euston Road, London NW1 3AQ	01-387 9951	●														
Aquamatic Showers, 152–154 High Street, Uckfield, East Sussex TN22 1AT	0825-3444								●							
*Armitage Shanks Ltd, Armitage, Rugeley, West Midlands WS15 4BT	0543-490253	●	●	●	●				●	●	●	●	●	●	●	●
ASL/Portashowers Ltd, 70–72 Hospital Street, Nantwich, Cheshire CW5 5RR	0270-64448							●	●							
Barber, Wilsons & Co Ltd, Crawley Road, Westbury Avenue, London N22 6AH	01-888 3461								●		●					
*Barking Brassware Co Ltd, 5–13 River Road, Barking, Essex IG11 0HD	01-594 7292								●		●					
Belco Manufacturing Co Ltd, 802 Park Royal Road, London NW10	01-965 2481								●		●					
Berglen Ltd, 29 Temple Fortune Parade, Finchley Road, London NW11 0QS	01-458 7133	●				●	●	●	●				●			
British Ceramic Tile Council Ltd, Federation House, Stoke-on-Trent ST4 2RU	0782-45147											●				
*Carron Co Ltd, Carron, Falkirk, Stirlingshire FK2 8DW	0324-24999		●	●	●				●		●		●			
*Chloride Shires Ltd, Guiseley, Leeds LS20 8AP	094 32-3232	●	●	●	●									●		●
Concentric (Fabrications) Ltd, Unit 4, Hawkesworth, Swindon, Wilts SN2 1DZ	0793-6756			●											●	
*Crayonne Ltd, Windmill Road, Sunbury-on-Thames, Middlesex TW16 7EE	76-85131	●				●										
*Curran Engineering Ltd, PO Box 23, Hurman Street, Cardiff CF1 1TH	0222-33644			●												
Dahl Brothers Ltd, Scandia Works, Molesey Avenue, East Molesey, Surrey KT8 0RY	01-874 4377			●					●	●						
*Deltaflow, Metropolitan House, 1 Hagley Road, Edgbaston, Birmingham B16 8TG	021-455 7141								●		●					
*Dimplex Ltd, Millbrook Trading Estate, Southampton, Hants SO9 2DP	0703-77717	●														
Dolphin Showers Ltd, Weir Lane, Worcester WR2 4AY	0905-29387							●	●							
Doulton Sanitaryware Ltd, Wheildon Pottery, Stoke-on-Trent ST4 4HN	0782-47001		●		●						●			●	●	●
*Dryad Metal Works Ltd, 40–42 Sanvey Gate, Leicester LE1 4BF	0533-27457	●														
Thomas Dudley Ltd, Dauntless Works, PO Box 28, New Birmingham Road, Dudley, Worcs DY1 4SN	0384-557 5411												●			
*Eaton Ltd, Yale Security Products Division, Wood Street, Willenhall, West Midlands WV13 1LA	0902-66911	●														
J & T Ellis & Co Ltd, Wakefield Road, Huddersfield, Yorks	0484-39521												●			
*Fordham Pressings Ltd, Melbourne Works, Dudley Road, Wolverhampton, West Midlands WV2 4DS	0902-23861			●									●			
Gainsborough Electrical Ltd, 105–107 Dollman Street, Birmingham B7 4RP	021-359 3232								●							
*Gardex Ltd, Bredbury, Stockport, Cheshire SK6 2RX	061-430 5269								●							
Gardom & Lock Ltd, Alflow House, 222 Soho Hill, Houndsworth, Birmingham B19 1AP	021-523 3311								●							
*James Gibbons Ltd, PO Box 22, St Johns Works, Wolverhampton, West Midlands WV2 4BX	0902-20401	●														
*Glass Fibre Laminates Ltd, White Lund Industrial Estate, Westgate, Morecambe, Lancs LA3 3BU	0524-68822			●												
*Glynwed Baths Ltd, 28 Brook Street, London W1A 3BD	01-449 8941			●	●						●					

		ACCESSORIES	BASINS	BATHS	BIDETS	CABINETS	SHAVER SOCKETS	SHOWER CUBICLES	SHOWER FITTINGS	SHOWER TRAYS	TAPS, VALVES & FITTINGS	TILES & FITTINGS	VANITORY UNITS	WC CISTERNS	WC PANS	WC SEATS
Gummers Ltd, Effingham Valve Works, Rawmarsh Road, Rotherham, Yorks S60 1RX	0709-64865							●			●					
*H H Electrical (London) Ltd, 253 Kilburn Lane, London W10 4BJ	01-960 3121					●										
Homeplan UBM, Avon Works, Winterstoke Road, Bristol BS99 7PL	0272-664611	●	●	●	●	●		●	●	●	●		●	●	●	●
*Ideal-Standard Ltd, PO Box 60, Ideal Works, National Avenue, Hull, North Humberside HU5 4JE	0482-46461		●	●	●				●		●		●	●	●	●
*IMI Opella Ltd, PO Box 216, Witton, Birmingham B6 7BA	021-356 4848										●					
IMI Santon Ltd, Somerton Works, Newport, Gwent NPT 0XU	0633-71711								●							
*Johnson Brothers (Hanley) Ltd, Trent Sanitary Works, Stoke-on-Trent ST1 3LN	0782-29581		●		●									●	●	●
Key Terrain Ltd, Larkfield, Aylesford, Maidstone, Kent ME20 7PJ	0622-77811										●					
*Lilly & Sons Ltd, Baltimore Road, Birmingham B42 10J	021-357 1761	●														
Mac-Dee Plastics Ltd, Edlington Lane, Warmsworth, Near Doncaster, Yorks DN4 9BR	0302-854551		●	●												
Matki Ltd, Berkeley Avenue, Reading, Berks RG1 6JL	0734-585335							●	●	●						
Marley Extrusions Ltd, Lenham, Kent ME17 2DE	0622-54366			●												
*Metlex Industries Ltd, 85 Sumner Road, Croydon, Surrey CR9 3BQ	01-688 1133	●	●	●	●	●		●	●	●	●		●		●	●
*Meynell Valves Ltd, Bushbury, Wolverhampton WV10 9LB	0902-28621								●							
*Modular Extensions Ltd, Netil House, 1–7 Westgate Street, London E8 3BR	01-986 3131	●														
Newman-Tonks Ltd, Hospital Street, Birmingham B19 2YG	021-359 3221	●														
Osma Plastics Ltd, PO Box 12, Rigby Lane, Dawley Road, Hayes, Middlesex UB3 1EY	01-573 7799													●		
*Ottermill Chilton Ltd, Church Way, Hungerford, Berks RG17 0JW	04886-2121						●									
*Pegler-Hattersley Ltd, St Catherines Avenue, Doncaster, Yorks DN4 8DF	0302-68581								●		●					
*Pilkington's Tiles Ltd, PO Box 4, Clifton Junction, Manchester M27 2LP	061-794 2024											●				
*Redring Electric Ltd, Redring Works, Peterborough, Cambs PE2 9JJ	0733-60431								●							
Reliance Foundry & Engineering Co, 37 Pomeroy Street, London SE14 5BL	01-639 7727										●					
*Roanoid Ltd, 1 Edison Street, Hillington, Glasgow G52 4UF	041-882 9031			●				●	●	●						
Robjo da Benton Ltd, 143 Grosvenor Road, London SW1V 5JD	01-828 1487	●							●		●					
*Sadia Water Heaters Ltd, Hurricane Way, Norwich Airport, Norwich NR6 6EA	0603-44144								●							
Shavrin Levatap Co Ltd, 6 Cannons Drive, Edgware, Middlesex HAN 8DN	01-952 2558								●		●					
*Sheardown Engineering Ltd, South Road, Harlow, Essex CM20 2AP	0279-21788										●					
*W & G Sissons Ltd, Calver Mill, Calver Bridge, Sheffield S30 1XA	0433-30791		●													
Sommer-Allibert UK Ltd, Berry Hill Industrial Estate, Droitwich, Worcs WR9 9AB	09057-4221	●			●											
*Strongbeam Co Ltd, Warwick Yard, Victoria Road, New Barnet, Herts	01-449 2407	●														
Topliss Showers Ltd, 18 Victoria Road, Tamworth, West Midlands	0827-62621								●							
*Twyfords Ltd, PO Box 23, Stoke-on-Trent ST4 7AL	0782-29531		●	●	●			●	●	●				●	●	●
*Walker Crossweller & Co Ltd, Cromwell Road, Cheltenham, Glos GL52 5EP	0242-27953								●		●					